# Keyspeech

## 9 Keys to Inner Power

*Learn the Secret Code to the Language of Success*

**Yvonne Oswald,** MHt, MNLP, MTLT™

Page layout & design, Gary Wein
gwein@shorecreative.com


Note for Librarians: A cataloguing record for this book is available from Library and Archives Canada at www.collectionscanada.ca/amicus/index-e.html
ISBN 1-4120-6400-7

*Printed in Victoria, BC, Canada. Printed on paper with minimum 30% recycled fibre. Trafford's print shop runs on "green energy" from solar, wind and other environmentally-friendly power sources.*

# TRAFFORD
**PUBLISHING**™

*Offices in Canada, USA, Ireland and UK*

This book was published *on-demand* in cooperation with Trafford Publishing. On-demand publishing is a unique process and service of making a book available for retail sale to the public taking advantage of on-demand manufacturing and Internet marketing. On-demand publishing includes promotions, retail sales, manufacturing, order fulfilment, accounting and collecting royalties on behalf of the author.

**Book sales for North America and international:**
Trafford Publishing, 6E–2333 Government St.,
Victoria, BC v8t 4p4 CANADA
phone 250 383 6864 (toll-free 1 888 232 4444)
fax 250 383 6804; email to orders@trafford.com

**Book sales in Europe:**
Trafford Publishing (uk) Ltd., Enterprise House, Wistaston Road Business Centre,
Wistaston Road, Crewe, Cheshire cw2 7rp  UNITED KINGDOM
phone 01270 251 396 (local rate 0845 230 9601)
facsimile 01270 254 983; orders.uk@trafford.com

**Order online at:**
trafford.com/05-1311


10  9  8  7  6  5  4  3

# Introduction

## Keyspeech - 9 Keys to Inner Power
### *Learn the Secret Code to the Language of Success*

This transformative book takes NLP to a completely new level. Get ready to change your whole perspective on life as you are empowered to accept joy and abundance as your birthright. Discover and develop clear communication skills, resilience and supportive behaviour that will take you to dynamic levels of success.

You'll tap into your own inner resources as you learn to use simple, flexible strategies of communication with yourself and others to ignite your passion and bring you to health, prosperity and happiness. Feel the excitement of the energy of words as you discover a new sense of magic and hope inside yourself, leading you to the joy and harmony of inner peace that we all long for.

The link which takes you from middle brain judgemental to the higher brain functions of endless possibilities is simply a matter of switching your inner and outer language. I call it Keyspeech because clearing your language of low-energy keywords releases an enormous amount of power for you to create the space to fulfill your goals. I know these winning techniques work because I hear from people daily about how their thinking and the results in their lives are magically changing as they use new resources and learn the language of success, leading them to celebrate life on every level.

Get ready now to tap the boundless potential of the universe by integrating the inner and the outer world. Follow the step by step process that will set you free.

Amazing results are guaranteed as you master the principles of the Nine Keys to Inner Power.

# Message from Yvonne

I have been working with people and doing life consultations and therapy for more than twenty-five years now. I remember being with my guide Peter during one of my early meditations. I was making a chair from white cane, in a small cabin in a valley. I knew that there were some more to make. "How many more are there?" I asked, as each chair seemed to take a long time. "Look out of the window" he said. I gasped as I saw what seemed to be thousands of partially made chairs, extending in a line as far as the eye could see. "I'll never do all those!" "One at a time," Peter said "one at a time."

Many years later I was with a client who had a long slow task ahead of her to get her life back on track. I used the story to explain to her that tasks had to be bite sized. I suddenly realized that we were sitting in those exact cane chairs that I was making in the cabin and that I had indeed helped to make many thousands of people's lives happier ever since, by facilitating their sense of self-worth and belonging.

I had a similar experience when I began studying Hypnotherapy.

Peter and I were standing near the ocean.

"What am I going to do with this new direction?" I asked.

"You're going to help all those people."

I looked along the long stretch of seemingly endless beach and there were people as far as I could see packing the beach thirty or forty deep.

"No way!" I exclaimed "That's too much for one person."

"Exactly" the guide said with a smile, "Let me show you how…."

He offered me a lit candle to light the one I suddenly had in my hand. As I lit my candle from his, I noticed four women and a man in front of me. Each one was holding a candle in one hand, which was extended towards me.

I lit the five candles with mine and they each turned and lit someone else's.

I watched in awe as the whole beach lit up in a wave expanding into the distance.

It was magical to see the faces light up with smiles as the light was passed.

"Now that I can do," I said with relief.

I now pass the light of the candle to you, knowing that you will feel just as honoured as I have, as you help people to find the light and the magic inside themselves.

# Contents

* * * *  With Thanks  * * * *

* * * *  Win Free Stuff  * * * *

* * * *  Yvonne Oswald – Bio  * * * *

# Why do you need to learn to use Keyspeech?

- Simply because your happiness and the results in your life depend directly on the efficiency of the flow of communication between your inner and outer mind. Great communication allows you to embrace life, trusting in the guidance of the greater power which we call God, or the Universal Mind. It allows you to accelerate your personal growth with an attitude of curiosity and experimentation, much as a child does.

You'll experience a profound change in your approach to life as you learn to enjoy its lessons and take the journey in a more relaxed way. The most important relationship you'll ever have on this journey is the relationship you have with yourself. To the degree that you love, accept and communicate with yourself, you'll attract success into your life accordingly.

The second most important relationship is your relationship with other people. Adjusting your communication style to enable others to like and support you and your goals allows you to feel empowered and in control of your life.

The awe-inspiring truth is that you can be anything you want to be, do anything you want to do, and have everything you want to have, by following a few simple rules. In order to tap into the amazing power which is available to you today, you first need to find out more about yourself and your place in the universe, and secondly learn a new language – the language of success.

Are your relationships constantly improving? Is your health good? Do you feel vital, fun-loving and alive? Are you prosperous? Do you feel connected and clear about the future? Are you contributing and feeling fulfilled? Do you love where you live? Are you ready to grow and change and willing to play the game 100%?

Great! Then let us begin:

# THE FIRST KEY –
## The Power of AWARENESS
### *Know Yourself*

*"I'm trying to free your mind, Neo. But I can only show you the door. You're the one who must walk through it."*

THE MATRIX (FILM) 'MORPHEUS'

Why is it important for you to understand yourself and be aware of your thought processes? Because you create your world with your thoughts and words. What you focus on is what you actualize, so your thoughts and language need to be clearly directed to produce great results.

## Will the 'Real You' Please Stand Up?

Who are you really? You have a name, but you are not your name. You know that you have a mind, but you are not your mind. You are so much more than that. You are a being with an infinite supply of life-force. You were born with an inherent possibility for greatness, because you are one with God, the Master Creator. You are the Master Creator of your own life.

Your individuality makes you unique, and at the same time as being an individual, you are part of humanity. Everything you say, think or do has an impact on your environment and on some level affects all the rest of us, however subtly.

So who else are you and how does what you do impact others?

# *The Crystal Universe*

## Good Morning, Starshine!

You are perfect! Let me explain...
Imagine yourself as a beautiful multi-faceted crystal:

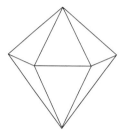

This crystal represents the blueprint for happiness that you already have inside you. Each facet represents a different aspect of your wonderful self: all of your talents, abilities, and present and future potentials. As you go through life, every experience you have has an effect on the surface of the crystal.
An unhappy experience might become a mark on the surface of one of the facets - perhaps one that represents 'self-worth'. A powerful experience, such as a time when you truly did the best that you could in spite of circumstances that were less than easy, would shine up a surface and allow the light of the universe to shine through and reflect from the crystal face, connecting you with God, or the Universe; the source of all intelligence, abundance and joy.

Eventually patterns form. Imagine that these patterns become 'printed' on the surface of the crystal. Unfortunate habits might become dark marks which stop absorbing or reflecting light. Good habits and right decisions allow the crystal to become more and more beautiful as facets attract and absorb more light. Whether you believe in God, quantum physics, or both, the unifying force or commonality is that light is life-affirming and absence of light is non life-affirming. An absence of light acts as a separation or disconnection from the source, which is the place where all abundance is accessible.

What does this have to do with you being perfect? EVERYTHING! Notice that I said the surface of the crystal, not the crystal itself. The crystal is the inner part of you which is unchanging, everlasting; you may call it God, the Universe, the Eternal Flame, the 'I Am' or anything else. It is the invisible blueprint of life. It is the part of you which is exactly like all the rest of us. It is neither 'good' nor 'bad'. It is simply perfect. Think of a power such as electricity. Electricity has no intrinsic quality of 'good' or 'bad'. It is just a source of energy. It does not 'think'. It just 'is'. However, it can be used for good or not. It can light up the universe, or be used in a less constructive way.

How you experience life can be viewed in just the same way. You can choose to use your own energy for great or uninspired results, depending on how you react to events that occur. Events in our life are just that - events. You can choose to respond to those events differently by paying more attention to them and feeling very thankful that you are being given signals and signs to help you along the path.

*Albert Einstein said: "God does not play dice with the universe."*

People who are 'aware' know that there is a pattern to the universe which is predictable and reversible. People who are 'unaware' believe that there's no such thing as free will. I believe that you're always on the correct path but some correct paths take longer to travel than others!

**There are those who know; there are those who don't know; and there are those who don't know they don't know!**

Every choice and every decision you make has a ripple effect on the Universe, like a stone being thrown into a pond. It is up to all of us to remember that individually and collectively we can effect enormous change for the total benefit of humanity and the planet.

*"It is one of the most beautiful compensations of this life that no man can sincerely try to help another without helping himself."*

EMERSON

You can now polish your own crystal and in doing so, help others to do the same to theirs. When all of our crystals are shiny and beautiful, the universe will light up, truly connected in truth and joy as we combine our light and form a vast ocean of loveliness – a quantum universe, where everything is possible.

# *Quantum Mechanics*

*"To Infinity and Beyond!"-Buzz Lightyear*

*"There is no reality in the absence of observation"*
THE COPENHAGEN INTERPRETATION OF QUANTUM MECHANICS

Classical Physics gives us a way to understand how the natural world works. It assumes that there is an order to things which, when understood, will allow us to have tools to make predictions about the natural physical world. However, during the first part of the 20th century, scientists were finding a whole range of extraordinary phenomena in their laboratory experiments that didn't seem to conform to regular rules of Classical Newtonian (action /reaction) Physics.

There was something extra that their old calculations didn't explain.
Scientists then began to formulate some acceptable theories for the unusual results which now form the basis for quantum mechanics. Quantum (from Latin quantus, or 'how much') Mechanics is the branch of physics that governs how the smallest particles behave. In this world, substance is nothing more than vibration and all that exists is particles and waves. Quantum Mechanics involves a significant reworking of the physical laws of behaviour at the atomic and subatomic scale, because at this level wonderfully strange things happen; for instance, an electron can be in two places at the same time.

Contributions were made by a whole group of scientists, resulting in a series of papers and lectures put together in 1936 in Copenhagen by Neils Bohr and Werner Heisenberg that is now more or less accepted as the 'orthodox' interpretation of quantum mechanics.

Its main features are that a property does not exist unless it is able to be measured and that it's not easy to measure because indeterminacy is a fundamental property of the universe (Heisenberg's Uncertainty Principle states that the more variables there are, the more unpredictable the result).
In other words, nothing is real until it's measured and there are things that we just can't measure but we know they exist because they have an observable effect on things we can measure!

Or more simply put, the whole is not the sum of its parts but is much larger. There is a hidden variable which does not allow us to measure results with any degree of certainty. This 'hidden variable' acts as interference and causes an entangled state.

Why is this important? Because the hidden variable is one of the keys to accessing a huge amount of previously untapped power.

Everything has a unique frequency which produces vibration, which in turn produces sound. Quantum devices tend to be more sensitive to noise than their classical counterpart. More powerful and accurate sensors, detectors and measurement devices are constructed as a result. The strangeness of quantum behaviour also gives rise to opportunities not usually available. At the level of the quantum field, which is the name given by scientists to the distribution of energy that is constantly creating and recreating particles, just about anything becomes possible.

Although you appear to be having a linear, localized experience, you yourself are non–local. You are so much more than you realize.

Your hand, while it is part of you, does not describe your whole body.
Look more closely though, at each cell, and the DNA in every cell is identical to every other cell in the whole of your body. Look even more closely, at the quantum space between each cell, the subatomic space, and you are looking at the stuff the universe is made from, making you both a microcosm and a macrocosm at the same time.

## As within, so without. As above, so below.

Your brain is the most exquisite device, which is available to you to shape this universe. It's an amazing organism.

*"It has 100 trillion possible connections, all capable of simultaneous calculation. And that's just for processing! It also holds the equivalent of twelve hundred terabytes of computer memory – six million years of the Wall St Journal!"*
THE FOOTPRINTS OF GOD – GREG ISLES

That being so, why is it that you haven't got everything you want instantly? Because the interference pattern caused by limiting beliefs and negative emotions needs to be cleared so that you can restore the mind to its true state of joy, harmony and trust. Then you can truly start to create your world.

*Remove the zero (or what is not) from Good and you get God.*

Your brain is not just an information processor. You are **so much more** than that. You are about to learn how to send and receive communication with clear intent and no interference. At the level of the quantum field, novel kinds of information exchange, processing and manifestation is then available to you.

Remember the hidden variable? This is where it comes into effect. As you learn to fine-tune and increase your sensory acuity, you'll find yourself in the magical world of quantum potentials, amazed at how quickly you can find solutions and change the results in your life. The Nine Keys are the tools you need to reach this state of evolving transformation.

You know, things are not always what they seem to be.

Imagine yourself picking up a book, opening the first page and reading it. Someone else can pick up the same book and read exactly the same information, as what is written remains the same. However, although it appears to be the same book, the second you picked it up, all the molecules you touched were changed. We live in a holographic universe (as within, so without), so every molecule affected every other molecule. By the time the next person read the book, it was a completely different book, although to all intents and purposes it remained the same.

As you were reading the pages, your impression of the world changed because you received more knowledge and formulated an opinion. The next person reading the same book may have a different perspective as a result of reading the same information! We all have a shared model of reality although all of our separate realities are not the same because we each have our own perspective. Our thoughts, beliefs and feelings affect the way we view the world.

If you saw the movie "What the Bleep do we Know?" you will have seen the water crystals frozen in time by Dr Masaru Emoto*, a Japanese researcher. He produced evidence to support the fact that thoughts, words and feelings actually affect physical reality. He presented written, spoken words and music to the same water samples, then used an extremely powerful microscope in a very cold room, along with high speed photography, to photograph the newly formed frozen water crystals.

*Two books: Messages From Water and The Hidden Messages in Water

He discovered that the crystals change when specific, concentrated thoughts are directed at them. Water from clear springs and water that had loving words directed toward it showed brilliant and colourful complex patterns like snowflakes. Polluted water, or water that had low-energy thoughts directed towards it, had dull coloured, asymmetrical patterns.

**Our world is 70% water. Our bodies are 70% water.**

Imagine, then, that your thoughts are just as real as your hand as you picked up the book (as in fact they are).What thoughts did you send out today? Imagine that your words are just as real (as in fact, they are).

As you begin to change your mind now and in the next few days, you can choose to see, feel, hear, touch, think and speak differently. Imagine, as you speak and think, how your words might affect water and then realize that those words affect your mind and body in the same way. Words have enormous energy and power.

I started using Keyspeech, replacing low-energy speech patterning with high-energy, life-affirming word patterns, more than a year before I had heard of Dr Emoto's work. Consistent speech and thought repatterning will introduce resonance and harmony to your life, preparing you to tune in to the higher frequencies needed to produce consistent, powerful (and quick!) manifestation of all your goals. View any and all events that distract you from your goals as feedback that you need to be more consistent. The question is not when are you going to decide to clear obstacles, but how quickly can you meet them and pass them?

Just imagine how your life is about to improve as you choose to change your responses to events NOW, as you begin to connect with and reclaim the immense power of your inner mind, opening the space for success.

Conscious decision-making is the first step towards creating your happy future because it opens up your beliefs to the idea of total freedom of choice. As you begin to move forwards, change then occurs at the unconscious level and results are instantaneous.

*"Those who believe they can do something and those who believe they can't are both right."*

HENRY FORD

The initial responsibility for change begins with…you guessed it…yourself! It's also wonderful when you *introduce* change rather than waiting for change to happen. In other words, do you choose to be *re*active or *pro*active?

Humans are, by nature, creators and creative. Manifestation of all your hopes and desires begins at the highest possible level of creation (God), vibrates easily through the superconscious / collective unconscious into the unconscious mind. The unconscious mind is directly in contact with this awesome power and the more the conscious mind connects, or is in congruence with the unconscious (and hence the higher self or super conscious), the quicker your desires will manifest.

That being said, it's important to know how you can access the unconscious mind and learn how to formulate suggestions in such a way that will make it listen and be encouraged to take an *active* part in your quest for a healthy, prosperous and happy life. To do that, you need to understand how the conscious and the unconscious* minds work:

## *Be Mindful of Your Conscious Mind*

The **conscious mind** consists of approximately 10% of your mind. It functions in a state of awareness. As you are reading this page, you become aware of the words on the page and its layout. You are using your logical, conscious mind to do this. The conscious mind initiates all the cognitive concepts: learned knowledge, verbal and mathematical skills, creativity and reasoning. This particular brain function comes into fruition at around the age of two, as you become more autonomous and self-aware.

The conscious mind controls all voluntary body movements and knows your body and its surroundings through your sense organs. All of your perceptual senses report to the conscious mind. We perceive the world consciously predominantly through five channels: sight, hearing, taste, touch and smell. Visually dominant people remember the world primarily from what they remember seeing. Auditory dominant remember it by the sounds they heard. Kinaesthetics will remember a smell, or what they felt, touched, or tasted. By opening up more of your senses you can increase your conscious awareness and become more in touch with yourself and with life.

*The only difference between the unconscious and subconscious is the spelling!

As you are reading, become aware of your body temperature and the room temperature and the feel of the chair or surface beneath you. Become aware of any colours around you and notice what you can clearly see or what is out of your immediate vision. Notice if there are any smells or odours around and if they are pleasant or unpleasant. Can you hear a clock ticking? Music? Nature? Traffic? Silence? How does your mouth feel and taste right now?

The conscious mind **gathers** and **sorts** information. In order to do the above exercise you needed to slow your reading down slightly in order to process the suggestions, but no matter how fast or slow you were reading, the information was gathered and presented to you at the speed of thought – amazingly fast.

Your conscious mind sorts out **probabilities.** If you decide to go out today, you will make a conscious decision about what to wear based on probabilities. If it's a beautiful day you would most likely wear light clothes. Being a **decision maker** and a **judge,** you may also take a jacket based on the probability that it may get cooler in the evening, and extra money just in case you decide to go to the cinema later on. As conclusions are reached, the conscious mind **presents information to the unconscious mind** for it to store and memorize.

Later tonight as you are walking along in the light jacket and the weather turns distinctly cold, you may store this information for the following evening, or even the following year, so that, based on new information received, the conscious mind can **retrieve information from the unconscious mind** and make a new decision to take a warmer jacket next time.

The conscious mind makes **generalizations.** As you stroll along, you may notice a cute animal. If it's got four legs, is hairy, is wagging its tail and barking, the conscious mind will conclude that it's probably a dog!

Your conscious mind likes to **analyze and categorize** to stop you from repeating patterns not to your benefit. However, the judgements that the conscious mind makes are only as good as the information retrieved from the storage unit of the unconscious mind, which could have filed away as many as 150,000 low-energy commands or warnings from parents or other authority figures before the age of seven!*

Your conscious mind uses willpower to make you act, but given that only 10%

*Anthony Robbins

of your mind is conscious, willpower alone is not enough to help you to succeed. If all it took was determination, we'd have all been successful long before now! Up to 90% of your mind is not conscious, so no matter how much you want to change, if the unconscious mind is replaying old videos, or memories of when you did not succeed, your results may be inconsistent. If your thoughts and actions are to be effective, your unconscious mind, where imagination lies, has to be in harmony, or in agreement, with the conscious mind.

So how do you change the inner mind? The easiest way is to access and clear from the unconscious mind any outdated programming that it may have held in its storage files, replacing it with powerful new programming, so that the conscious and unconscious mind act in accord, forming a congruent under-standing. The more synchronization that takes place, the more quickly your desires become your reality as you access the higher levels of consciousness. You will also find that you become a clearer and more powerful conduit of healing for both yourself and others in your life.

We will be using some NLP techniques and Hypnosis to lead you to these higher levels of consciousness. NLP and Hypnosis are both sciences which study the way the mind works. NLP (Neuro Linguistic Programming) is a set of techniques based on modeling results-oriented methodologies of excel-lence. It's the study of subjective experience and how it affects our behaviour, both physiologically and psychologically. Hypnosis* is a delightful state that you naturally go in and out of every day... when you're watching TV and are thinking of something else, or when you're lying in bed imagining your wonderful future of amazing possibilities. Science has confirmed that Hypnosis is a means of connecting the body and the mind and as such is a powerful tool for change.

*All hypnosis is self-hypnosis.

# *Recap*

**The conscious mind**
1. Is aware of what it perceives
2. Is in contact with reality through the sense organs – touch, sight, hearing, smell and taste
3. Can communicate with the universal conscious or superconscious (God) only through the unconscious mind – **has no direct link when low-energy thoughts or limiting beliefs are present**
4. Sorts out information in order to send it to the unconscious mind to store
5. Tests probabilities in order to decide what action to take – can think deductively (you think something)
6. Makes generalizations – can think inductively (makes you think)
7. Is a decision-maker and a judge
8. Reviews and judges information, draws conclusions and presents those conclusions to the unconscious mind for storage
9. Requests information from the unconscious mind – often from deep inside

**Your Unconscious -Mind**
This is an invitation to take an exciting journey into the realm of your unconscious mind. Why do you need to know how your unconscious mind works? Because it controls 90% of your functioning and successful results in your life. The unconscious mind is basically anything other than conscious.

The conscious mind is like the computer operator and the unconscious mind is like the Internet; but unlike the Internet, the unconscious has some prime directives (purposes) that it has to perform, the most important one being that of keeping the physical body healthy and functioning.

**How can I get my unconscious mind to work with me towards some wonderful happy outcomes?**
By realizing that the unconscious mind is similar to the Internet. The unconscious mind draws conclusions only from information in its storage memory. Unlike the conscious mind, which can draw conclusions from what is not said or apparent, the unconscious mind can only produce results based on the way the question or information is presented to it by the conscious mind.

If you've ever tried to find a site on the Internet using keywords, you'll understand how this system works. Type in the word 'boxes' and you'll get anything from candy boxes to coffins. I was searching last week for an 'alpha stimulator' and up popped all kinds of sex sites ('stimulate' can have other connotations than the meaning I had intended)!

The unconscious mind has opinions based on the programming by the conscious mind. Once you make a conscious decision, the unconscious mind believes to be true any conclusions that are based on that decision. After that, no matter how much willpower the conscious mind uses, over time the unconscious will eventually reassert itself and present results based on previous programming. It needs to be reprogrammed by the conscious mind, or convinced that it is healthier to change, in order to proceed differently.

The unconscious mind also cannot differentiate between reality and imagination, and as the conscious mind is 100% reliant on the unconscious, even the conscious mind has no easy time deciding what is 'real'.

The unconscious mind, which is also where manifestation begins, is made up of fundamental drives (genetic and collective) and memories. With repetition of actions or thought processes, habits are formed. Habits are useful in that they allow us not to have to reprocess every bit of the two million pieces of information which enters our brain every second. They enable us to make generalizations and expectations; rather like when we learn to drive a car – all the new information is a little much at first, but eventually driving becomes totally automatic. Driving another car takes just minutes to get used to because cars, although slightly different in their make-up, have generally the same format in the way of gears, steering wheels, wipers etc.

If we start to believe that a memory or habit is a fundamental drive, then that becomes our truth and subsequently our reality. For example, by continually choosing relationships that are not easy, we may make the assumption that 'All relationships are not easy', and that becomes its own self-fulfilling prophecy and part of our belief system, and hence our reality.

When we add in the fact that 'reality' is totally subjective (ask three people to describe a dramatic or emotional occurrence and you may not think that they were talking about the same event!), you have the likelihood of inconsistent results.

The bottom line for successful results is right thinking; decisions made by repeating previous actions which turned out well. Before right thinking (then right action) can occur, awareness is the key to change. You can't change something that you don't know about!

**Awareness**
plus
**Availability of choice**
(I always have a choice!)
leads to
**Adaptation**
(new ideas/creativity/learning)
to allow
**Absorption/Assimilation**
resulting in
**Action**
(purposeful action based on purposeful results.)
leading to
**Active participation in life!**

How do you become aware of what the unconscious mind needs from you in order for it to supply your needs? You learn how it works. The good news is that you can reprogram the unconscious mind simply by understanding the instructions it needs in order to produce high-energy and directed output. The pictures, sounds, words and feelings you use to communicate with yourself shape what you perceive to be your reality. By consciously using words you can consciously create the reality you want and deserve. You have at your finger-tips, in the unconscious mind, an immense amount of previously untapped resources that are just a thought away.

As we go through the functions of the unconscious mind point by point, you may formulate different ideas about the way you speak and think for the future, so that your conscious and unconscious minds can begin to work together as a team or partnership. You will be amazed at how quickly a sense of peace and trust begins to grow in your life. You'll also be delighted at the way your desires become reality almost immediately as you clear away previous patterns.

# *The Secret Code to the Unconscious Mind*

Your unconscious mind is programmed to seek more and more as it moves towards wholeness. It's designed to give you what you focus on.

**1) Health connection – Your Health is truly your wealth.**

Your unconscious mind's NUMBER ONE directive is to operate and preserve the physical body, so ALL suggestions to do with keeping the body healthy and protected are immediately accepted, remembered and acted upon. Sometimes it comes to conclusions that it believes are for your protection which you need to uncover and release in order to get better emotionally or physically.

Ask yourself: "What secret is my unconscious mind holding for my protection that when it is released will allow me to become my magical, more healthy, authentic self?" just before you sleep at night and trust your unconscious to respond. You may have an interesting dream or find that an unusual event the next day will give you a clue.

The unconscious runs the body's autonomic nervous system, which includes respiration and breathing, the heart, the immune system and digestion. Anything in fact that keeps the body running efficiently is the domain of the unconscious mind. However, our conscious thoughts can affect that smooth-running system. Low-energy thoughts have been proven, by Kinaesiologists doing muscle testing, to produce weaker muscles. High-energy thoughts can produce stronger muscles. A recent U.S. study with elderly people in bed with long term disabilities proved that just thinking about exercising leg, arm and body muscles for only ten minutes a day actually improved the muscles' strength and appearance in less then a month.

Your thoughts affect every cell in your body, so true healing takes place primarily mentally *before* the physical manifestation occurs. Only last week I used this health connection to stop a migraine. I have not had a migraine for years now, since I began hypnotherapy, so as I awoke at 2:00 am with that less than good feeling that everyone who ever had a migraine would know starts a three day cycle, my first reaction was one of surprise. However I knew that I had been putting in many hours to make a big health show successful, so I sat up and said aloud: "I want to thank my unconscious mind now for reminding me that I have been over-doing it. I am listening and I am aware and I'd like to tell you right now that this is not in the best interest of my health, as I still have two days' work ahead. So to keep me healthy, I suggest that you let go, relax and help me to sleep well tonight. Thank you." I lay down (*without* taking any drugs). Ten minutes later my head was clear and I had a great sleep.

By connecting with the idea of health, any suggestion will be looked upon with interest by the unconscious mind.

I stopped my husband snoring simply by reminding his unconscious mind that, as his metabolism was increasing, his airways would be clear and he wouldn't have to snore anymore as it is healthier to breathe deeply and clearly in sleep! He hasn't snored since (and this after eight years of every attempt to stop, including those nose strips to keep nostrils open!).

Be careful how you talk to yourself – the word 'diet' to the unconscious mind implies lack of food. Food is essential for the body to stay alive, so planning a 'diet' will most likely result in many trips to the fridge to stock up! Suggesting: "I love to eat fruit and vegetables now because fresh food makes me slimmer and therefore healthier", is a much better way to persuade the unconscious mind to join in the quest for slimness.

Could you find ways to get rich by using a health connection?
How about: "I am rich and wealthy now because prosperity allows me to relax more and so become healthier!"

Be as inventive and imaginative as you can – your unconscious loves suggestions that are given in a fun way, because they keep the conscious mind occupied and out of the way while the unconscious is making changes.

## 2) The Unconscious mind has a direct connection with the Super-conscious/Collective Unconscious/God/ Universal Consciousness.

Edgar Cayce, the Sleeping Prophet, used to say that the use of 'imaginative forces' is the key to spiritual awareness. The altered states produced by hypnosis, prayer, meditation and simply the use of imagination open a doorway and direct link or connection to the higher self and higher power, resulting in 'miracles'.

# *The Window to God*

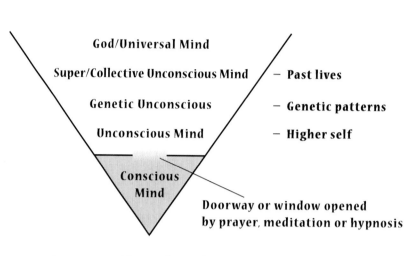

God/Universal Mind

Super/Collective Unconscious Mind — **Past lives**

Genetic Unconscious — **Genetic patterns**

Unconscious Mind — **Higher self**

Conscious Mind

Doorway or window opened
by prayer, meditation or hypnosis

– Access to guides and angels and wishes coming true.

Once the doorway is fully opened, a simple request is enough for a miracle to occur. I see and experience miracles almost daily. It's wonderful to watch a client become 'reconnected' and step into a desired state of health or happiness simply by becoming aware that they are part of something much bigger than they thought, perhaps by going back to a pre-birth or previous lifetime experience.

3) **It stores and organizes memories – it remembers *everything* – a very useful tool if used in a directed way.**

I remember an experience with my father when I was 14 years old. He had a burning pan of fat and was walking towards the back door, his hands burning as the flames got higher and higher with the fresh oxygen from the doorway. Without thinking I grabbed a tea-towel, soaked it in water and threw it on the pan, dousing the flames immediately. I have no recollection of when or where I learned that trick, but both of us were very glad that my unconscious mind had the memory somewhere and stored it for later use.

Every second your brain processes 2 million pieces of information. As the information is being internally represented, it is filtered down to 134 bits, then down again to around 7 chunks. Tad James* likens this to 2,000,000 toothpicks falling from the sky, from which we can grab a handful of 134, which we then tie into bundles of 7.

*Advanced Neuro Dynamics, Hawaii

During the process the information is generalized, sometimes becoming distorted or deleted before it is stored and filed. A current experience may trigger a memory and a response then takes place, using the recalled memory as a conscious means to judge what should be the appropriate action. If the memory is stored efficiently and no distortion occurs, then the result is as easy as remembering how to ride a bike. However, if emotions are involved in the storage or retrieval of a memory, unexpected results can occur:

4) **Your unconscious mind stores and operates emotions, suppressing negative emotions, which it will present to the conscious mind to resolve at a later date.**

Emotions are at the root of our behaviour. They are the driving force behind motivation and behind any decision to take action (people generally drive toward pleasure or away from pain). Emotions stored in the unconscious are the most powerful emotions, as they surface when 'triggered' by a current event. Both pleasurable and not so pleasant current events can trigger previous memories.

The role of the unconscious mind is to manifest the emotion that is most appropriate to what is happening in the current event or experience.

However, if an event is strong or overpowering, the correct emotional response may not immediately register, as the 'fight or flight' survival mechanism kicks in. If the unconscious mind feels that survival may be compromised, or some kind of threat is imminent, or even if the emotional response is simply too much (as in grief at the death of a loved one), then appropriate emotions may be put to one side in order for the person to just 'get by'. Dissociation is the result, which is an excellent temporary protective mechanism.

Later, these stored emotions may get triggered at an appropriate (or inappropriate!) time, as the unconscious mind will take any opportunity to release these unwanted memories, rather like you or I would be happy to clear out cupboards full of old stuff. 'Forgotten' memories can surface in the form of impulses and compulsions. We may not even know why we act as we do, because the memory that triggered the compulsion is still hidden. Food can have emotional ties to comfort or love, which can trigger overeating to stimulate endorphins in order to keep us 'balanced'. However, overeating or less healthy eating leads to even further imbalance and a cycle is created.

## 5) Your Unconscious Mind Maintains Genealogical Instincts

Anything instinctive is usually a genetic memory: eating, sleeping, reproduction and glandular function are just a few of the instinctive patterns which allow us to lead more efficient lives.

The 'fight or flight' survival mechanism is an instinctual memory which is a response to stress. It's hardwired into our neurology and is primarily a protective device. Our ancestors needed to respond to a surprise attack by either fleeing or fighting, both of which needed a burst of energy to the body to provide a means for survival.

Unconscious thought processes which served a useful purpose were stored and utilized in the form of impulses. Cravings are part of the instinctive need of the body, which used to be valid thousands of years ago, when our ancestors craved food, went out and hunted, brought it home to prepare it or cook it and then felt satisfied. These days we in the Western World have no real need for cravings, as food is always available. We are aware of the need to eat, go to the fridge or cupboard and eat. Even before the craving is complete (usually around two or three minutes) we have already taken steps to satisfy it. Then before the brain can even register that food has been eaten (around twenty minutes) we want more and do it all over again! A simple way to stop this pattern is to eat protein around 11am, *before* the hypothalamus stimulates the desire for an instant sugar fix by producing galanin*.

## 6) It Creates and Maintains Least Effort Patterns.

Habitual behaviour is easily established. Once learned, you can comfortably direct your attention elsewhere and just run the program. Driving a car is a perfect example of a habitual behaviour pattern. By automatically knowing how to *mechanically* drive a car, the conscious mind is freed, ready to instantly learn any new information presented in the way of unusual road conditions or other drivers' behaviour.

We call all these habitual behaviour patterns 'routines' and a routine is a useful, easy pattern to establish, with obvious constructive benefits. An example of an unfavourable routine is that of the instant gratification of snacking while watching T.V., or staying in a job just because it is 'comfortable'. This behaviour can be changed by a powerful push from the unconscious mind. Studies

* "Breakthrough Body Kit", available through my website at www.hypnonow.com  has many other tips on quick ways to achieve a slimmer, healthy body.

show that it takes just 21 days to establish a new behaviour pattern or habit. A habit is an acquired behaviour that is repeated until it becomes almost involuntary. There's a tendency to think of 'habits' as unfavourable. In fact, beneficial habits are just as easy to establish as unfavourable ones!

**7) It communicates with symbols – uses the language of metaphor and imagination to create the future in partnership with the conscious mind.**

Your thoughts are metaphors or symbols representing your experiences, which the unconscious mind presents in the form of imagery. A model or map of the world is formed by each individual, which is used to guide behaviour. Being purely subjective, every choice we take makes sense when viewed in the context of our own model. If we are to understand our experiences, then these models will guide us. Sometimes these models do not serve us. They may become less flexible, leading to incorrect choices being made, or they may become uncreative, leading to no choices being made. To greatly expand your growth-producing choices you just need to increase your imagery and imagination and formulate clear intentions followed by action.

**8) Your Unconscious takes direction from the conscious mind and will only accept suggestions from someone it respects – which could be why your unconscious mind doesn't listen to you sometimes! How is your unconscious mind possibly going to want to follow your suggestions unless you love and respect yourself?**

Both the unconscious mind as well as other people believe about you what you believe about yourself. Your self-worth is truly the foundation for your belief and manifestation of a great self-image, success and happiness. How many times have you praised yourself today? How many rewards or gifts have you given to yourself? How do you talk about yourself?
Which reminds me – how do you talk about other people?

**9) Your unconscious mind accepts things literally and personally.**

Be careful what you say about other people because your unconscious mind thinks you're talking about YOURSELF, so your self-worth may not be as great as it could be because your inner mind accepts all your words as the truth. One way to change this is by switching your key words, which leads me to number…

**10) It doesn't process negative commands.**

Do not think of a white elephant. Do *not* think of a white elephant with pink spots – dancing, on a stage. Do *not* remember the number 167. Which number are you not to remember? Your unconscious cannot process what is not. It simply responds to the key words you give it.

Feel this:
a.) And now, just thinking about all the tension and tightness in your shoulders, all the day-to-day worries and concerns, relax your shoulders and just let them go.
Where is your imagination right now?

Alternatively, feel this:
b.) And now, just thinking about your shoulders, relaxing them, releasing and imagining a beautiful pink energy like liquid light flowing down and through the shoulders, softly, softly letting go…o…o.

Please be aware of these two examples as you speak to other people in your daily life.

# *RECAP*
## The Unconscious Mind:

1) Operates and preserves the physical body –PRIME DIRECTIVE
2) Has a *direct* connection with the superconscious/collective unconscious/god/universal consciousness
3) Stores and organizes memories – it remembers *everything*
4) Stores and operates emotions (suppressing strong low-energy emotions to present to the conscious mind to resolve at a later date)
5) Maintains genealogical instincts
6) Creates and maintains least effort patterns
7) Uses metaphor and imagination to create the future in partnership with the conscious mind – communicates with symbols
8) Takes direction from the conscious mind – will only accept suggestions from someone it *respects*
9) Accepts things literally and personally
10) Does not process negative commands

You might think of the *conscious* mind as a 'Word' document, which receives all words with no response. Think of the *unconscious* mind as the Internet which recognizes and processes the *key* words in a sentence and responds by showing you all other chains of words and meanings stimulated by each key word. Negative words have been proven to produce low vibration or energy and positive words produce high vibration or energy.

Living in Canada, I hear people say "No problem!" when they really mean "You're welcome". Just think what the unconscious mind actually hears! It doesn't process the 'no' and it just hears 'problem'. I just went to my computer and keyed in the word 'problem' - 21,200,000 websites came up! Your unconscious mind is a billion times more powerful than any computer yet invented. How many chains of meaning, memories or events were triggered by that one word?

There is actually a word to describe this process: litotes!
(pronounced: lie – toe – teez)
The dictionary describes litotes as:
*An understatement in which an affirmative is expressed by negating its opposite.*
Even the explanation is not easy to understand.

In fact, by changing the low-energy key words to high-energy ones, you can actually change your mind!

"It's hard" becomes "It's not **easy**"

(The word 'hard', by the way, brought up 91,600,000 websites!)

"I'm broke" becomes "I'm not **rich**"

"I'm afraid" becomes "I have no **courage**"

"I'm sick" becomes "I'm not very **healthy**"

The result of changing your language provides a wonderful solution to clearing your mind of non-productive inner talk. Observe how the unconscious mind hears those sentences:

"It's (~~not~~) easy"

"I'm (~~not~~) rich"

"I have (~~no~~) courage"

"I'm (~~not~~) very healthy"

Yes, it's a whole new language and it's a wonderful way to introduce yourself to the whole new you who is ready to emerge, fresh and smiling, into your happy, successful life.

# THE SECOND KEY –

## The Power of CHOICE and CHANGE
### *Choice and change bring freedom*

The reason you can choose to change is that change is a dynamic force which propels you forward into life. Conscious change creates a space to move beyond what you thought was possible and come into your full power as a human being.

## *This is the Dawning of the Age of Aquarius*

Why has change happened so rapidly this past century? Note that the Vietnam War began about thirty-three years before we entered the Age of Aquarius in the year 2000. This thirty-three year period was the 'cusp' period as the planet entered into its next astrological cycle after the last two thousand years of Pisces. Vietnam was really the first time that people questioned why war was necessary. Since then, we've seen the Berlin wall come down and we've seen remarkable changes in Russia and the Middle East. Communication and technology have developed at a phenomenal rate.

Jesus was said to have lived thirty-three years; his death marked the end of two thousand years of Aries (the sequence of astrological ages moves backwards in two thousand year periods) and the beginning of the age of Pisces. Pisces is the communication sign of the Zodiac and is also the sign of duality; its symbol is represented by two fishes swimming in opposite directions.

The age of Pisces was a time of awareness of separation from the source, a time of Authoritarianism in most western civilizations. The church used to be the ultimate authority figure. Indeed, at the Council of Nicaea in 325AD, most of the references to reincarnation were edited out of the Bible because believing in past lives took away from the power and authority of the church (Jesus said, "I am Abraham" - that was one they missed!). These days the church is becoming much more approachable as people begin to find their voices and have more say.

It is fitting that Albert Einstein was a Pisces. His ideas became the bridge between the Age of Pisces and the Age of Aquarius, combining science and philosophy and changing the way we understand the functioning of the universe. His was the single most powerful force that led us to question ideas about the meaning of energy and time.

Gerald Holton, of Harvard, stated that: "There were no boundaries or barriers between Einstein's scientific and religious feelings. He lived under a compulsion to unify – in his politics, in his ideals, even in his everyday behaviour."

This is a wonderfully exciting time to be alive. We are in an era of Aquarian oneness and equality. Aquarius is a time for each of us to take personal responsibility. It's a time when we learn to co-operate and realize that we alone are accountable for events taking place on our planet because we are all part of the collective unconscious which we call 'God' (the Big Crystal!).

## *Are We There Yet?*

What can you change? Anything and everything that is not working well for you! Flexibility opens up new choices. Many years ago, when I began to counsel people, I used to feel that there were hundreds of queries about life's choices. I sat down one day and actually wrote them on paper. I was surprised at how few there really are. This is the list I compiled:

| | | |
|---|---|---|
| Life's purpose(s) | Birth | Fears |
| Career | Creativity/hobbies | Past Lives |
| Home | Relationships | Death |
| Money | (partner/spouse, | Self- image/growth |
| Health | friends, colleagues) | Travel |
| Family | Spirituality | |
| (parents, siblings, | | |
| children) | | |

I'm sure that you can think of a few more. What I realized though, is that most of these subject areas require no actual change. They simply require further knowledge or a change of perspective. You cannot, for instance, change your family. You can only change yourself and your reaction to it.

What you *can* change will bring balance, harmony and self-empowerment into your life, which will ignite your passion and result in a life of success.

## The Seven Areas to Change

### HEALTH, CAREER, FUN AND RECREATION, MONEY, HOME, RELATIONSHIPS, SELF- WORTH

If you feel that you are not in a position to change any of these seven, then the only thing left to change is your ATTITUDE!

Do you remember that the Prime Directive of the unconscious mind (which is 90% of the mind) is to keep you healthy and alive? Let's start the changes with a look at your health.

When people talk about their health they're usually referring to their physical bodies. But we actually have four bodies that we need to keep healthy:

> Spiritual
> Mental
> Emotional
> Physical

You have a body, but you are not that body. You are not your thoughts, nor your feelings. You are a powerful, constant source of infinite light energy with the ability to heal yourself on every level. You have innate, radiant inner beauty and strength with a natural sense of values to inspire you towards seeking love and knowledge.

## *Your Health is Truly your Wealth*

As you get older it becomes apparent that your health is one of the most important things to value in life. Currently there are 230,000,000 Internet sites devoted to it. The actual word 'health' is derived from the Anglo-Saxon word 'hale' (as in 'hale and hearty') meaning whole, complete. 'Holy' has the same origin. That being so, there must be a connection between being healthy and being connected to spirit, or to God.

I like to think of it as being one with life, being one with yourself.

The interference and eventual separation that occurs when people are not at one becomes disease. Disease of the human body or mind is exactly that: DIS-EASE. In other words, a blockage or imbalance in one or more of the four bodies causes discomfort, eventually lowering the immune system.

How do you release negativity and move towards ease and health? The first step is to change your internal and external speech patterns. Be prepared now to learn a new way of talking to yourself as you free your internal and external dialogue using KEYSPEECH!

## *KEYSPEECH*
## **Change your Words,**
## **Change Your World**

Your unconscious mind is a vast sea of knowledge, rather like the Internet. The knowledge is out there all the time but unless you go and sit down, turn on the computer and make the connection you may not even be aware of the mass of information available to you to help you find solutions to become successful and happy. That connection is made more easily with your inner Internet if you clearly say or think your intention in dynamic words that state what you want.

Your unconscious mind takes no personal interest in anything you say unless it relates directly to health or survival. It also stores and retrieves every chain of meaning associated with every single word you utter and every thought you think. It's been scientifically proven that low-energy thoughts lower the immune system and make you more illness-prone. In a BBC News study published in 2003, researchers from the University of Wisconsin – Madison measured the electrical brain activity of 52 people aged between 57 and 60. Those with the highest levels of activity in the right pre-frontal cortex (the pessimists) hardly responded to a flu vaccine. Those with the strongest activity in the left pre-frontal cortex (the happy thoughts people) had much stronger immune systems and produced many more antibodies in response to the flu vaccine.

## BEING HAPPY ADDS 9 YEARS TO YOUR LIFE!

In general, people are either motivated by moving towards something good or away from something not good. Do you always think about getting out of debt or do you think about making money? Make it your goal from now on to be always moving forward towards a great healthy future.

Notice that I said 'not good' instead of 'bad' earlier? If you type into the Internet the word 'good' you get 186,000,000 websites available to you. If you type in 'bad' you'll find 78,000,000. In your mind, those websites represent all the memories and chains of meaning associated with the words. If you think of the word 'good', your unconscious mind retrieves every memory around the word 'good' – Do you remember every good thing that ever happened? Your unconscious mind does and will remind you of every good incident simply by your focusing your attention on the word.

Think of the word 'bad' and it does exactly the same. Remember all those bad times? Exactly! Not a nice feeling associated with that word is it? Remember about the chains of meaning when you use any low-energy keywords

If you think of 'not good', it doesn't have the same squirmy effect in your stomach as the word 'bad' does it? That's because your unconscious mind cannot compute something that is not! If you think of electricity, it is simply a power. It does not think. It is neither 'good' nor 'bad', and it can be used constructively or not. So it is with your thoughts. The internal representation of thoughts also resonates throughout your body, ultimately affecting your immune system. Your goal is to constantly direct those thoughts into high-energy by switching your internal and external language.

Young children act rather like the unconscious mind as they respond to the keywords you give to them. Just try telling a child not to do something! "Don't touch that!" A child's immediate response is to reach out and touch unless the command is given in a strong tone which implies danger (the child's unconscious mind overrides at this point because of the health or survival mechanism).

The use of the word 'NOW' is important to your unconscious mind, because if you think or say the word 'now' it's like pressing the 'ENTER' key. on your keyboard.
It makes the connection occur and action follows.
Every parent knows this!

"Katie, turn off the T.V. please"
"Katie, turn off the T.V. – we're leaving"
"Katie, come on!"
"Katie, turn it off" "**NOW**!!" – action!!

Here are some common phrases that have been switched:

That's not **bad** –       That's quite **good**
No **problem**    –     You're very **welcome**
That's **bad**     –     That's not **good**
Don't **worry**    –     You'll be **fine**
Put some **effort** into it    –    Let's put some **energy** into it
It's too **hard**    –     It's not **easy**
I'm **sick**      –     I don't **feel well**
I **forgot**       –     I didn't **remember**
I've been **working hard**    –    I've been **working well**
Don't **cry**      –     It's **okay**. I **know** ............

This last switch is an interesting one because the child (or adult)'s conscious mind can do a mind read in order to release the emotions associated with the crying i.e. It can understand "It's okay to cry" or " It's ok – you're safe". "I know" can be translated as "I know how you're feeling" or "I know the solution".

The language structure of Keyspeech is not very elegant right now. However, as we begin to use our cerebral cortex more, I believe that new and more elegant language will begin to emerge as people realize the effect that words and their meanings have on our psyche. Words and thoughts are real. They translate into pictures or images in the unconscious mind. The process of thinking occurs twenty-four hours a day, seven days a week, so it's important that your inner voice and imagery remain harmonious and flowing. It is important to remember that your unconscious mind cannot differentiate between an image that is real and an image which is imaginary.

Let me give you an example:

I was driving to Niagara Falls with a friend from England some years ago, a trip I usually really enjoy. As we drove (on a wider highway than she was used to in England) she began to get uneasy.
"Oh my God, this **traffic** is **terrible.** Look at that **idiot.** He's going to **hit us** if he's not **careful. Watch out!**" (Her foot pressed on her imaginary foot pedal) "Whew! That was close. There must be **loads of accidents here** the way they drive. It must **worry** you **sick.**"

By this time my heart was pounding, my hands were sweating and I had my eyes bulging out of my head! In actual fact, the man in the other car had simply passed our car on the inside lane, which is not legal in England, so my friend's fears were unfounded. The words underlined were what my unconscious mind actually heard. I finally told her to stop talking and asked her to surround our car with a wonderful protective light! Images of angels of protection were in my head for the rest of the journey.

Your mind thinks in images or symbols, so structure your language to create images in your mind about what you want to happen, or what you desire.

## Savings in Your Thought Bank

High-energy keywords are equity in your thought bank and contribute towards good health. Low-energy words do the opposite.
Firstly, find the low-energy keywords and limiting beliefs in this conversation:

"Good morning John! How are you?"
"Not bad, not bad. I was pretty sick over Christmas and I'm still trying to shake it off. I always get sick at this time of year. It's depressing."
"Poor you! That sucks. Did you get that flu that's going around? It's a really nasty one this time. Everyone's catching it —it seems to last for weeks because you think it's gone and then it comes back. It's hard to get rid of. Anyway, I've

got the book you ordered. It's a bit expensive - $25 I'm afraid."
"Oh! I'm a bit broke right now so do you mind if I get the money to you after
I get paid next week, or will a post-dated cheque do?"
"Don't worry. I know it's really hard right now. The economy's always down
every January. Whatever works for you is fine."
"Thanks very much, Linda." "No problem. See you later." "Bye!"

There are at least nineteen low-energy keywords (and depending on the tone
of voice used, there could be many more), and two limiting decisions (example
– "The economy's always down every January" – not necessarily true but it's a
nice excuse for not managing money well!).

Key in some of those low-energy words to the Internet and you get a phenomenal number of search results. Beneath every word there is a conscious and
unconscious chain of meaning. At best the high-energy keywords simply
replace the low-energy ones, leaving you with no equity in the thought bank.
Too many low-energy words take you into negative equity, which lowers your
immune system and impacts your health. Not very cheerful news. However,
let's re-do that encounter using all high-energy keywords and leaving out
limiting decisions:

"Good morning John. Are you well?"
"Actually, I'm much better. I was not well at Christmas so I've decided to get
healthy for the New Year."
"Great! I wish you success. I've got terrific news for you – the book you
ordered has arrived. It's $25."
"Wonderful! Can I collect it next week? I'll have more money by then!"
"Sure! Whatever works for you is fine. I'll see you soon."
"Thanks a million Linda." "You're very welcome John." "Bye!"

Notice how much more economical language becomes when the low words are
not there. Productive keywords propel you forward and upward as they
resonate to a much higher frequency.

**Equity in the Thought Bank**

The Internet is a representation of our holographic universe and a product of
our collective minds, therefore it follows logically that the Net is a propor-
tional representation of what we think about.

Just for fun I entered the keywords from the two conversation examples into the Internet and the results were very interesting!

**1St Conversation:**

| | | | |
|---|---|---|---|
| GOOD | 376,000,000 | BAD | 134,000,000 |
| PRETTY | 61,000,000 | BAD | 134,000,000 |
| MONEY | 242,000,000 | SICK | 24,700,000 |
| WORKS | 146,000,000 | TRYING | 78,000,000 |
| FINE | 90,400,000 | SHAKE | 11,400,000 |
| THANKS | 114,000,000 | SICK | 24,700,000 |
| | | DEPRESSING | 4,330,000 |
| | | POOR | 4,100,000 |
| | | SUCKS | 7,470,000 |
| | | FLU | 7,300,000 |
| | | NASTY | 12,100,000 |
| | | CATCHING | 6,950,000 |
| | | HARD | 167,000,000 |
| | | EXPENSIVE | 28,500,000 |
| | | AFRAID | 17,600,000 |
| | | BROKE | 17,200,000 |
| | | WORRY | 23,200,000 |
| | | HARD | 167,000,000 |
| | | PROBLEM | 196,000,000 |

TOTAL: **1,029,400,000**          TOTAL:  **1,065,550,000**
(Life-Affirming, high-energy words)    (Non Life-Affirming, low-energy words)

This conversation is in negative equity! That's why you don't feel great when you talk with someone who's not happy.
Every word has its own individual frequency and low-energy words have been proven to have a lower frequency than life-affirming words. The higher the frequency or vibration, the better you feel.

Energy and vibration levels are also raised by chanting, sounding and singing, which is why we sing or chant in church. Singing, in fact, has been proven to boost the immune system, promote optimism and improve physical health by improving breathing capacity*.

Here are the search engine results from the second conversation:

2nd Conversation (low-energies edited out)

| GOOD | 376,000,000 | SURE | 148,000,000 |
| WELL | 361,000,000 | MILLION | 111,000,000 |
| BETTER | 213,000,000 | WELCOME | 233,000,000 |
| WELL | 361,000,000 | TERRIFIC | 8,520,000 |
| HEALTHY | 43,100,000 | WONDERFUL | 42,000,000 |
| NEW | 1,580,000,000 | SUCCESS | 90,500,000 |
| GREAT | 347,000,000 | | |
| WORKS | 149,000,000 | | |

TOTAL: **4,063,120,000** Life-Affirming Keywords

You're a thought BILLIONAIRE!

Success in the bank, as your mind has direct access to the generative effect of high-energy thinking. It's time now to get more "Yes's" inside.

## KEYSPEECH SUMMARY
### -SWITCH!

1) Always talk and think about what you want your results to be; clear intent, using high-energy words. Your words are gifts that you give and receive.

2) Think of every word you speak as though it's a keyword you're typing into the Internet. What results would you get back? What results are you getting from the keywords you are thinking?
   If you catch yourself saying something with low-energy, replace it immediately (think 'switch!'). e.g. "I feel horrible today." (switch!) –"I don't feel great."

3) If you find it less than easy to replace a low-energy word such as

*Researchers at Newcastle University, UK

"challenge" e.g. "I'm finding this a challenge" replace the word with "interesting" – "I'm finding this … interesting."
You'll have many interesting sentences coming out of your mouth soon!
Another switch sentence is "I've got a great opportunity for growth." or, "I'm learning some lessons right now".
'Puzzle' is also a good switch word.
"I'm looking for a solution" works very well.

4)  State what something is *not* on purpose.
    e.g. "This is really hard. It's a problem." becomes (switch!)
    "This is really not easy. It's making me think."
    By thinking 'switch', you automatically go into high-energy Keyspeech.

5)  Speak in the now as though it has already happened
    (and be realistic so that the conscious mind believes that it's possible).
    "It's easy for me to have a wonderful relationship now"
    or "I am ready for a wonderful relationship now"
    (Rather than: "I will have a wonderful relationship." The unconscious mind is happy to believe that a wonderful relationship will happen sometime in the future, so there is no direct need for it to respond).

6)  Whenever you are planning something that you want to succeed, add a 'health' connection. "My new venture is successful now because with more money in the bank I can relax more and be healthier."

7)  Use the words 'because' and 'now' as often as you can.
    The conscious mind likes the word 'because', because it answers the question "Why?"
    The unconscious likes 'now' because it's like pressing the word 'enter' on your keyboard. It jumps straight into action.

8)  Clear "Don't" (do something) from your dealings with other people
    e.g. "Don't drop that on the floor." Switch to: "Hold that carefully."

9)  Clear 'have to', 'could have' and 'should' from your self-talk
    "I should do my work now."
    These words imply obligation – resentment on some level is the only

response. Switch to: "I'm ready to do my work now."

10) Clear the word 'try' from your vocabulary – we use the word in hypnosis to make sure someone fails! "I'm trying to be successful" Switch to: "I'm more successful every day".

11) Clear 'but' from your vocabulary. 'But' can imply judgement. Replace it with 'and': "You did that well but you need to correct the spelling" becomes: "You did that well and perhaps you can just check your spelling?" 'But' is also a word that's usually followed by an excuse for not making changes: "I'd like to exercise, but……"

12) Switch your language! Make a pact with your children, spouse or friends to catch each other and switch the language. We have a points system with my daughter – she wins 10 points if she catches us. It's very rare that I can catch her!
"Don't worry Katie!"
"Switch the language mom." "You'll be fine Katie!"

13) Make a point of consciously using high energy words such as gratitude, laughter, kindness, love, abundance, success, joy, freedom, power, and health in your everyday speaking and thoughts. Choose one word, write it, use it, act on it and live and breathe it for the whole day.

## *Key Speech Body/Nutrition Words*

Diet: eating plan or nutrition plan
Fat: not slim
Junk food: empty filler food
I'm feeling guilty about eating: How interesting that I chose chocolate to eat.
I shouldn't be eating this cake: I wonder why I'm eating this empty filler food?
I was bad today: I didn't do very well today. I'm better from now.
I'm depressed: I'm releasing some emotions right now.

Have fun finding replacement phrases. It takes a short time to make it work so that you go straight into the high-energy space without going first into the low-energy. It's very much like learning a new language*. Initially you translate from one word or phrase to another and then it becomes automatic. How do you know when you're changing? Proof that Keyspeech is working is when you become happy when people point out your low-energy words! At that point, you are truly approaching the paradigm shift that will take you to clear your language and bring fabulous changes to your life.

Change is something that some people find less than easy to initiate. While fate brings opportunities, free will is what we do with those opportunities.

Free will involves the need to initiate change by making new decisions.

How do you make decisions with ease and learn to trust your inner mind?

Let me show you how simple it can be:

## Easy Decision - Making 1-10

At 42, two months after the birth of my first and only child (an 'aged prima', the doctors called me!) I was extremely hormonal and not functioning well.

I went from being a very capable woman to a person who could just manage day to day tasks. Sometimes not even those!

One day Will (my husband) asked me to look up a phone number and my reply was, "I can't do that today." I really meant it. My day was mapped out in small steps to allow me to cope and finding a phone number appeared to be a big task! Decision-making was even more interesting. I found I could not prioritize. The day I discovered my 1-10 method, I had a babysitter for the first time for two hours. I couldn't make up my mind whether to go shopping or swimming. Twenty minutes later I was still sitting, asking "Shopping or swimming? Shopping or swimming?"

Finally I snapped out of it by thinking,

"Okay, Yvonne, give me a number between 1 and 10 (one being low and 10 being high): Which would do me more good, shopping or swimming? Swimming-7/ shopping-4. Swimming it is!"

I started applying the method to simple decisions like what I would have for breakfast:

"Toast-7, cereal-2. Toast it is."

I found that it worked for everything- so much so that I was also able to apply the method to more important decisions. I know that my soul or unconscious mind 'knows' much better than my conscious mind the state of the universe as

* Please feel free to contribute Keyspeech switch words to Yvonne@hypnonow.com

it applies to my needs (not desires), because it has my best interests at heart.

Do this method on simple decisions at first, like "How good is it for me to have pasta tonight?" (1-10)

**5 or below, the answer is NO.**

The quicker you get the answer, the more you can trust it.

"How good is it for me to…" is far better than "Do I want to…?" Yes, you may want to marry Jim (or Mary), but would it be good for you? That could be an entirely different matter.

How you ask is extremely important.  Say: "How good is Jim for me at the moment?"  You may come up with a 7, which means that he is teaching you something (even if that something may not make you happy!), or that he is really good for you right now. "How good will Jim be for me in 5 years' time?" It may go down to a 4, which means that it is not a matter of if, but when the relationship will end, so it's not leading anywhere. Check out all your friend-ships with this method. You may have interesting results.

"How good is my job for me right now?" Five or below, start looking elsewhere for another one, because you're already past the leaving date!

Don't trust your intuition yet?  Try this method every day for a month for small things like, "What do I need for lunch?"

| | | | |
|---|---|---|---|
| Sandwich | 3 | Fries | 4 |
| Pasta | 2 | Soup | 8 |
| Salad | 7 | | |

Ok then-salad and soup it is.

Another way to begin the question is to ask, "How likely is it that…..?"
I find this phrase very useful for financial decisions, for example, "How likely am I to make money from this new venture?" (1-10)

Enjoy learning to trust your decision-making ability. After just one week, you'll be much more in touch with what your body and spirit needs and your instincts will be improved.
The most successful people in life make decisions instinctively and act on them

quickly. Researchers at the University of Herfortshire in England concluded that high achievers almost always act on their instincts better then anyone else.

You now have the first two keys to Inner Power. As you become more self-aware and more able to adapt and make changes quickly, your health will improve because intuition, optimism and action will become a natural, everyday part of your life. True, vital health and peak performance comes when you are balanced on every level: physical, mental, emotional and spiritual. This next key is the one key which is essential if you are to find inner peace and happiness. It's the key which is about to lead you to self-worth.

# THE THIRD KEY –
## The Power of SELF - LOVE

Why is self-love so important? It's important because loving and accepting yourself means that you can share intimacy with someone else, which is something that we all desire on some level. It's often been said that your relationship with someone else can only work if you have a good relationship with yourself. You need to feel worthy of receiving and be able to celebrate who you are to achieve intimacy.

How do you know if you love and accept yourself? For the next week (or for the rest of your life), simply observe the kind of people (or events) you attract in every day. Life is purely a mirror, a reflection of what you feel and believe about yourself now and what you need to believe.

If you meet someone who is angry, ask yourself "What am I angry about?"
If you meet someone happy, congratulate yourself.
If you meet someone who is being successful, enjoy his or her success and praise yourself, because you must be doing something right!
Even if you are not sure that life is a mirror, acting as though it is assists you in becoming more objective about your choices.
You are the initiator of everything in your life.

## *Change Your Internal Language*
## *It's Time to Make Friends – With Yourself!*
### *Write your own script in only 10 minutes*

The true language of success begins with self-worth. Are you ready to write your own self-love script? It's the one about the authentic you.

Do you truly know your best qualities? How do you find out? Read on!

For the following exercise: Please write the lists numbered 1-7 on a separate piece of paper.
You'll need a hand held tape recorder or karaoke machine for recording your own voice, the voice your unconscious mind loves to listen to the most!

Make a list of the best qualities of your mother (even if she's not here), as though you are speaking to her.
For example: emotions, talents, practicality, looks, intelligence, people skills, determination, sense of humour, education etc.
State it like she is (no low-energy words).

1. You are _____, _____, _____, _____, _____, _____

**Make a list of the best qualities of your father.**

2. You are _____, _____, _____, _____, _____, _____

**Who is the person or animal you love the most? Best qualities:**

3. You are _____, _____, _____, _____, _____, _____

**Who or what kind of people do you most admire in the world? (Can be someone you don't know, for instance someone famous)**

4. I admire you because you are     _____, _____, _____, _____
                                     _____, _____, _____, _____

**Describe your ideal romantic partner:**

5. You are _____, _____, _____, _____, _____, _____
You are also _____, _____, _____, _____, _____, _____

**What things do you most admire about yourself? Look in a mirror, if you need some ideas with this one:**

6. You are _____, _____, _____, _____, _____, _____

**Now list 10 things or people you are grateful for in your life today.**

7. I am grateful for ___, _____, _____, _____, _____, _____
                     ___, _____, _____, _____, _____, _____

because...........................................................................

This is that basis of your script for the authentic you. What you notice and like in other people are your own best qualities.

Speak and record into the tape recorder (very slowly, counting 1, 2 between each sentence):

*As you close your eyes, relaxing more deeply than you've ever relaxed before, imagine yourself in a beautiful safe place in nature. Feel your face softening as you breathe and just ……let …go. There's a gentle breeze playing with your hair.*
*Perhaps imagine yourself in a forest, where there's water bubbling from a nearby brook, or by a lakeside, where a stream gushes over rocks to meet the lake.*
*Make your way to the water and you may be surprised to find, as you observe your reflection, that you seem to have a new glow around you. This is the real you, the authentic you. The sun is shining and there's a rainbow of light arching down from the sky, shining through the water droplets.*
*If you were now to imagine an angel or God as a colour, what colour would that be? (Pause)*
*Notice now how a shaft of this glowing colour is washing your entire head, shoulders and body with a new feeling of health and vitality as you become aware of how radiant you look today.*
*And you know as you reconnect now with that inner and outer light that you are that light. You have the knowledge and wisdom of eternity in every cell of your body.*

(Now read aloud your 1-6 results, all the best qualities of yourself)

*1. You are…*
*2. You are…*
*3. You are…*
*4. I admire you because you are…*
*5. You are also…*
*6. You know you are…*

*As you remember the authentic you, the true, pure, original you, you may recognize your inner spirit of truth and bravery. You may recognize the strength of character, honour and trust again, now.*
*You are breathing, you are living, you are relaxing into pure joy as you remember now a time in your life when you truly like yourself. Just one moment when you know that you are doing something admirable.*

*(Pause)*

*If you were to find a place in your physical body right now where that wonderful memory is stored, where would that be? (Pause)*

*Bringing your awareness to the one cell holding the most of that memory, observe, see, feel or sense a whirling vortex of power spreading outwards from that one cell, reminding each and every cell in your heart, chest, liver, lungs, and whole body of this delightful feeling.*

*Observing now every cell high-fiving every other cell in your ....shoulders, neck, head, face, arms, and hands. The intensity spreading now through your organs, spine, hips, thighs, knees, calves and feet – every cell singing and celebrating with release and freedom.*

*With pride and a delicious sense of satisfaction you notice that every cell in your whole body is tingling with excitement. Life is wonderful.*
*You realize suddenly that you are grateful. You are grateful for sunshine and laughter.......for the trees, birds and flowers.*
*You are blessed.*
*You are grateful for ....... (insert word list- number 7)*

*You can trust yourself now.*
*And now it's time to thank your unconscious mind for respecting and honouring you for all these years, asking it to continue the great work.*
*And perhaps the unconscious mind may want to gently prompt and remind the conscious mind to remember to change all language to life-affirming language prompting healthy suggestions for self-esteem and fulfillment.*

*Just before you drift off into a deep, deep sleep every night you may be reminded of something nice that you did today.*
*Perhaps you may remember something good that someone said about you.*
*Perhaps, however you sleep, deeply or peacefully, dreaming or not dreaming, you may awaken every morning feeling great, fully revitalized on every level, knowing that today is a new chance to start afresh, to begin something new. Today is a day to live life with laughter and fun, delighted to be alive.*
*It's a day to remember to love and accept yourself - now, only when you are ready, open your eyes to a brand new you.*

You may decide that "I am…" works better for you than "You are…"
This is just personal preference. Simply choose the language which you enjoy listening to the most. You can also add in any other suggestions to make you feel great.

Listen to this every day and you'll very quickly start to think of yourself in a whole new light.

*********************************************

## *Let go, let flow! Learn to Say No!*
## *-and then Reward Yourself!*

Self-love also involves being able to set boundaries.
I've studied palmistry since I was a child.
I'd say that 80 % of my clients have a 'resentment bulge" in their hand, formed by years of saying "Okay…." when they really mean:
"No, I so don't want to do that!"

Just inside the lifeline, which is the line on the inside of your palm going around your thumb to your wrist, feel with the second finger of your other hand. You may actually see a bulge, or just feel what almost feels like gristle, just below the surface (it looks like a worm). This area is called the Mount of Mars and should be very flat. If the resentment bulge is present for a long time it depletes the immune system. So let's clear it away.

You may or may not change your personality overnight, so here's a step-by-step method to learn to say no:

"Sue, could you please come and help me move on Saturday?"
Sue thinks "Oh no!  Not in my wildest dreams!"
Sue says, "Of course, it will be a pleasure. I'll arrange the babysitting and bring some hotdogs and we'll have a barbecue later!"
Sue thinks, "I can't believe I said that!"

Sue will do the job, end up feeling displeased and then disappointed if her friend doesn't even offer to pay for the hotdogs.

<u>Way Out:</u>    "How good is it for me to….?" (1-10)

**5 or below, the answer is NO!**

**Option 1: (1-10 decision)**

Sue thinks: "How good is it for me to help Ann move house?"
Response: 5 or 6 out of 10 (not a good enough response to spend the whole day doing it!).
Sue replies: "Okay – I can give you around three hours. Is from 1 – 4 pm okay? I need to get back home after that."

She has now shortened the time so that Ann can probably get someone else to do part of the work. Ann is too busy to thank Sue with flowers or a card – she's moving house and we all know how interesting that can be, without having to think about whether a helping friend feels validated!

Sue needs to reward herself.  Kids do it.

If I say to Katie, "Go and tidy your room Katie please", her immediate response is "Then can I play with Tayler?" (watch TV? have a treat?).  The reward is immediate.  Tomorrow is not an acceptable answer.  So as Sue responds, her reward should already be formulating in her head: a walk, a massage, a hot bath, a glass of wine.  It immediately lets the friend off the hook so that no resentment can form.  If Ann later remembers and comes up with the flowers or thank you note, it's received as a bonus, not an essential part of the equation.

It's important to allow yourself solitude every day to replenish your soul and make the connection with the inner mind. Take time for yourself in order to keep the well full. Do you remember that on an airline the instruction is given to make sure that you put on your own oxygen mask first? That's because when you feel great you have so much more to give to other people. For those of you who don't like to ask for help, just think how good it feels to help someone else when they ask for help, and give others a gift by allowing them to feel just as good by helping you.

**Reward List**
1. Walk or jog in the fresh air
2. Listen to music
3. Hot tub / facial
4. Massage
5. Pedicure
6. Eat something sensual "I eat this with love!"
7. New clothes
8. Book a trip
9. Feet up for 10 minutes
10. Special TV program
11. Glass of wine
12. A show or theatre
13. Dinner out
14. Walk around the house naked!
15. A swim
16. A work out
17. Hot sex (or self-service if there is no partner or significant other!)!
18. Learn something new
19. Read a book
20. Play golf / buy yourself a new driver
22. Sign up for a course
...and so on.

**Option 2**
Sue thinks, "How good is it for me to help Ann move house?" Response 2/10. If she still finds herself saying "Yes", the reward needs to be very big in order to console herself for doing something that she really doesn't want to do (a new set of clothes, a day off, three hours of doing nothing, a cinema / theatre outing).

The best response? "Oh Ann, Saturday doesn't work for me." ("I can't" only leads to "Why not?" and Sue will find herself not telling the truth!).
This is the halfway stage to learning to say "No".

After just a short time of practice, you will find that "No" becomes a word that just pops out one day. It's a very liberating feeling. By defining your boundaries, the time you would normally spend doing things with a heart that's less than open is returned to you, like a gift to yourself. This time can be used to replenish and boost your internal state. What do you do with all this extra time? Have fun and enjoy yourself!

# Optimism and Mood Boosters
## Quick tips to... Rela-a-ax

1) BREATHE
Take four deep breaths, anytime you remember. Close your eyes, holding each breath until the count of seven before releasing.

2) Begin the day with as much daylight as possible – open curtains to boost your serotonin levels for the rest of the day.

3) Play with a dog or pet – proven to increase serotonin levels. A robotic dog has the opposite effect*.

4) Keep real plants around you. They clean the air and raise emotions.

5) Start the day with fibre such as all bran or raisin bran. It helps to regulate cortisol (the stress hormone).
Orange juice (or any Vitamin C drink) has the same effect.

6) Remember the happiest moment of your life and imagine where that moment might be stored in your body if you have to choose a place. Then find the one cell that's holding that the most of that moment in your body. Imagine the cell as a little smiley person high-fiving every other cell throughout your body.

7) Snack on fruits with high levels of magnesium to boost your mood and keep cortisol levels down. Peanuts, almonds, sunflower seeds, and apples contain high levels of magnesium.

8) Doodle while you work – this sends your brain into alpha, which is similar to a state of meditation. It takes you into more peaceful higher brain functions.

9) Eat a banana. It contains B Vitamins, the first to be depleted when

*University of Missouri–Columbia study

stress occurs. B vitamins relax the nervous system and regulate the adrenals. Bananas also contain potassium, which is great for the heart.

10) Calcium (in the form of calmag (calcium magnesium) or caltrate for absorption) taken before bed at night relaxes muscles and helps sleep. Calcium is also known to improve depression and increase resistance to cancer.

11) Sing! The sound waves trigger alpha relaxation and the breathing changes encourage your brain to take time off. Taking singing lessons also improves your breathing and self-confidence.

12) Dance to music. In fact, any kind of fun movement will stimulate serotonin levels.

13) Meditate or do self-hypnosis for 15 minutes everyday.

14) Laugh. Be happy. Watch a funny movie.

15) Keep your chin up. Literally. This puts you physiologically into the higher brain, the happy brain. To remind you, look at a blue sky or hang a beautiful picture with some blue in it above eye level wherever you normally spend most of your day.

16) Stand up straight, look up, take a deep breath and hold it as you tense every muscle and think or say "Yes! Yes! Yes!"
Then release and let go.

17) Hunch your shoulders to your ears as you take a deep breath in, close your eyes and let go with a loud sigh.

18) Hug someone you like (or love).

19) Change your routine – stimulates optimism.

20) Reward yourself daily with music, a book, or other non-edibles.

21) Write ME in your daily schedule to remind you to take time for yourself.

22) Pray – Prayer has been proven to help release negativity. Studies show that weight loss dramatically increases when people pray.

The following NLP exercises change either your internal state or your outward physiology so that you can access feel good feelings at will:

1.  This is a great way to get happy fast.
    Close your eyes and remember a time when you felt really powerful. See what you see, feel what you feel, hear, taste and smell. Breathe it, be it. Feel the picture come alive. Now imagine standing outside the picture and shrink the picture down to the size of a small dark postage stamp. Send the stamp out to the top left hand corner of the room. How do you feel? Now as you say ZOOM! aloud, bring the picture back and imagine yourself stepping back into it. Feel the powerful time again and breathe it until you feel tingly and alive, then repeat, shrinking the picture and imagining zooming back into it a few times until you feel great.

2.  Change your physiology by standing up, shoulders back, breathing from the top of the lungs, eyes up and take a few deep breaths of release. This puts you instantly into high brain / happy brain/ alpha.

3.  Another way to access feel-good feelings is to close your hand in a fist and think "Yes!" anytime that you are experiencing fabulous fun or just feeling great. When you do this regularly, at some later time when you may be feeling less than good, just by closing your fist you go immediately to a place of feeling fine. This is called a resource anchor, in NLP terminology.

These short exercises get easier the more often you do them. Feeling wonderful about yourself and about life is a habit which is established very quickly.

## Finally, Prioritize and Praise Yourself

Write down your daily 'to do' list and tick off three essentials to do that day. Which are the three most important ones? When you've done those, count any other tasks that you accomplish as a bonus and tell yourself how amazing you are at the end of every day! This gives you a whole new perspective on life as you regain a sense of self-worth and pride in your accomplishments.
I've actually got my essential list down to one job with everything else as

praise, praise, praise!

Let's go on to the fourth key, which is about bringing the physical and emotional bodies into balance and harmony by releasing unwanted toxins and clearing negative emotions in order to reveal the new you.

# THE FOURTH KEY –

## The Power of LETTING GO and FORGIVENESS

Why is it important to let go, forgive and have compassion for yourself and others? Because true health and happiness is achieved by remaining in a constant state of joy, optimism and gratitude, which is not easy if a person is holding on to old low-energy states or feelings.

You can easily achieve a temporary optimistic internal state, as you have just discovered. However, for permanent change to take place, you also need to establish underlying behaviours to support the state. Before you can establish new behaviours, you need to first of all clear out the old ones to bring you to an optimum level of health.

### *The Key to Healing is to Release the Past-Spring-Clean Your Body and Mind*

Let's take a few moments to thank the body and the unconscious mind for being there and for loving us all these years. Every minute, every hour of every day, every week and month, year after year our body and mind have worked well together to keep us healthy and alive despite any low-energy patterns that we tried to sustain. Loving us unconditionally, always knowing what to do to help us regain balance and power.

Conventional medicine suggests that we are healthy until a bacteria or virus makes us unhealthy, whereas in fact we come into contact with millions of 'germs' every day with no apparent effect. Why is it then that not everyone is affected by these germs? The better your spiritual, emotional and mental condition, the healthier your physical body will be.

How healthy were you when you were at the best point in your life – in love or doing well financially or simply enjoying being alive? And how quickly did you not feel well when your life seemed to be less easy?

Stanley Burroughs in 'The Master Cleanser' points out that: "These germs and viruses exist in excess only when we provide a breeding ground in which they can multiply. Germs and viruses are in the body to help break down waste material and can do no harm to the healthy tissues." He goes on to say that all germs are friendly in that bacteria and viruses have the effect of assisting us to eliminate waste materials or toxins (in the form of vomiting or diarrhea) or mucus (colds/coughs). The lack of appetite that accompanies the 'disease' assists the body in healing as it can devote its time to breaking down toxins and waste.
I find that idea fascinating.

## You are not the same person you were this time last year!

Your body is the most wonderful mechanism. It replaces 95% of your cells every year. It regulates your temperature, sorts and carries hormones, enzymes and nutrients to the perfect location at the correct time. It replaces your skin every month, your stomach lining every 5 days, your entire liver every 6 weeks, your whole skeleton every three months. The 60,000 miles of blood vessels transport blood cells (and new ideas) every 20 minutes completely around your body.

Let us start by clearing out physical waste that may have accumulated in the body. It's advantageous to clear out initially on the physical level because your mind, body and spirit can work more efficiently without toxins.

## Therapeutic Fasting – Spring-Clean Your Body

Ancient Rome was the first ever Metropolis, with a population of over one million people and architectural and social achievements that are only being surpassed today. The Roman Empire stretched across one sixth of the surface of the globe, with a population of around 60 million. However, disease carried off 50% of those born before the age of 10. Of the rest, average life expectancy was roughly 25-30 years.

Average life expectancy today, with our attention to cleanliness and health consciousness, is well into the seventies, so how can we keep our bodies healthy and lean well into the later years? One of the real keys is therapeutic fasting, or cleansing. The practice of fasting has its origins in religion dating back to the beginning of recorded history. The purpose of religious fasting is purification of the body so that repentance can take place. Christians, Jews, Muslims and Buddhists, as well as various other sects regularly fast in order to access higher states of spirituality.

**In other words, if you are toxic on a physical level it interferes with the communication and thinking of the higher mind.**

In ancient times, fasts were begun at the vernal and autumnal equinoxes, primarily with the idea of increasing fertility, both of the land (symbolically) and of the body for reproduction.

*"Toxic overload sets the stage for many health challenges. The majority of the world's population cleanse for good health. By following their example, we could be healthier and slimmer. Cleansing is the key to permanent weight loss."*

DENNIS HARPER DO, SALT LAKE CITY, UTAH

It has now been discovered that there is a solid scientific basis for fasting, one of the main benefits and side effect of which is quick, easy weight loss and fat reduction. Children on a healthy supportive eating plan are full of life and energy, with a strong immune system. As we get older some of us tend to eat more than we need. Any amount of overload of food in your body results in the collection of waste products between the cells. The effects of this low grade toxicity can be tiredness, headaches, fatigue, arthritis, irritability and insomnia, not to mention less than good digestion, constipation, skin disorders, backache, gallstones, obesity, stiff joints, menstrual issues and a lowered immune system, all of which contribute to less clear thinking.

If any of these sound familiar, READ ON!!!
Your body needs plenty of water to help it run efficiently and two constant

sources of fuel: oxygen and food. Oxygen is taken in and utilized immediately by the lungs. Food, in order to enter the bloodstream, needs to be broken down into single molecules of fat, sugar and protein. As food enters your digestive system, bile and acid pour into your stomach to make the solid food into milky liquid called chyme. The liver and pancreas further break down and filter the nutrients, sending them through the small intestine for absorption into the body.

Nothing larger than one molecule can enter directly into the bloodstream for utilization by the body, with the exception of some small polypeptides (two to three amino acids together) and a little emulsified fat, as the intestinal tract only consists of a single layer of cells. These one molecule simple building blocks of life are called fatty acids, sugars (glucose, fructose, maltose etc) and amino acids. The nutritive molecules travel around your bloodstream and are pumped around by your heart through arteries, veins and tiny capillaries so that they can be used on an as need basis by any cell in the body.

Although your whole body is made up of billions of cells, every one of these cells has its own special job to do. What is most amazing about each cell is that its job is to work for the whole organism (the body). It 'knows' what it has to do, even if it involves sacrificing itself for the greater good (as in the case of the white blood cells).

Each cell 'talks' to other cells via an electrical messaging system which utilizes minerals and chemicals. These chemical messengers are called neuro transmitters. They bathe every cell in your body and are constantly eavesdropping on your nervous system, meaning that when you have happy thoughts, you have happy cells. Every cell has a plasma membrane which keeps it separate and allows it to regulate its own metabolism. The membrane is permeable but on a selective basis; it allows in only some of the molecules and atoms it comes across, not allowing entry to others.

All your cells have another thing in common: they are constantly working, building and breaking down nutrients. This breaking down process produces a 'soup' of waste products – mainly carbon dioxide, urea and uric acid which the plasma membrane excretes into the circulation to be carried out of the body via the lungs, skin, kidney and intestine.

This is where it gets really interesting! As the toxins gather inside each cell, ready to be excreted, the cell membrane senses the condition of the circulatory system. If the concentration of toxins is too high outside the cell, the cell will imprison its own toxins until conditions outside improve.

The body will also produce as many fat cells as it can to imprison the toxins in order to help keep the bloodstream and lymph moving. The more food eaten, even if it is burned up by exercise, the more waste is produced, the more a condition of low grade toxaemia is created in the body. As each cell becomes a storage unit for unusable toxic molecules it is less able to do its job efficiently, resulting in a system overload.

*"The body naturally manufactures fat in abundance to incarcerate and absorb chemicals and toxins that accumulate over time. As you cleanse the body of the toxins, one can expect fat and inches to be subsequently reduced."*
JK PAULSON, MD AMERICAN SOCIETY OF BARIATRIC PHYSICIANS

No matter how much healthy food you eat at this point and no matter how many vitamins and minerals you take, the body is locked into hanging onto the toxins (and fat cells) until such time as the system is more alkaline and more clean.

How do you clean your system?
Have you ever cleaned the oil filter on your car?
Have you ever cleaned the filter in the heating system in your house?
Have you ever cleaned the filter in your coffee maker?

The filtration areas of your body are the lungs, liver and kidneys, so let's start by de-congesting these organs. As you cleanse, a bonus side effect is that low-energy emotions are also released. According to the Chinese, the most important organ is the liver, so........

## *Learn to Love your Liver*

According to Chinese medicine, the organs of the body are a team, with the liver the master builder or chief of operations, second only in importance to the heart. Although the heart is essential for life, it is basically just a complex pump.

The liver however, performs over a hundred functions. It purifies two hundred litres of water every day and is also the most emotionally sensitive organ. Under stress, anxiety is produced. The liver responds to this by tensing; its vitality and regular functions are repressed, resulting in possible constipation, insomnia, nightmares and hormone imbalance (the liver is the single most important organ for hormone regulation- many 'women's problems' are caused by too much oestrogen being stored in the liver).

Chinese medicine tells us that depression is a sign of blocked liver energy. Louise Hay* calls the liver the 'seat of anger and primitive emotions'. Painkillers and drugs are absorbed by the liver and kidneys, often causing long term damage without conscious awareness. Calmag (calcium/magnesium) is an excellent pain reliever which allows the liver to remain healthy. One in twelve Canadians has liver disease**. People with a liver disorder commonly suffer from nutritional deficiency as most nutrients pass though the body without being assimilated if the liver is weak or congested. Autoimmune diseases such as arthritis, diabetes and allergies are often caused by a weak liver and spleen.

Every year in North America, a half million people in the U.S. and more then 50,000 Canadians have their gall bladders removed. According to the American Liver Foundation, the surgery to remove the gall bladder is the most common operation performed in hospitals. About 80% of gallstones cause no symptoms and remain asymptomatic. The following cleanse is excellent for releasing gallstones naturally.

Let's begin then, with a quick clean up of the gallbladder and liver (ideally do this Friday night, Saturday and Sunday – just make sure that on day 2 you are near a washroom all day!).

* Louise Hay – 'You Can Heal Your Life'
** Julia Chang www.sensiblehealth.com/gallbladder

# Gall Bladder and Liver Cleanse*

Mix 1         4 tablespoons of Epsom Salts ( from bulk buy stores)
              + 3 cups of water
Put in the fridge to cool overnight

Mix 2         1/2 cup light olive oil               (do not mix
              2/3 cup freshly squeezed grapefruit        yet)

---

DAY 1 4pm    Stop drinking and eating
      6pm    Take 3/4 cup mixture (1), then drink 1 mouthful of
             ordinary water (to make the taste better!)
      8pm    Take 3/4 cup mixture (1), then 1 mouthful of ordinary water.
      10pm   Get ready for bed, lie down and mix the olive
             oil and grapefruit juice well (mixture2).
             Drink in one go, then lie on your back for 20
             minutes.  Sleep all night.

DAY 2        Eat and drink normally (light foods)
             **Physical Release:** diarrhea
      8 am   take 3/4 cup of mix (1)
      10 am  take 3/4 cup of mix (1)

You will go to the bathroom most of this day.  Take a flashlight and shine it into the toilet bowl.  Anything which floats is a stone or developing stone.  The stones actually look like peas! Sometimes the release looks more like bran flakes or chaff (you may feel some nausea if you have many toxins in your body).

DAY 3        Emotional Release
             Morning: sometimes anger
             Afternoon: sometimes depression

DAY 4        Feel great- loads of energy!

Step two is to have a series of colonic irrigations.  Western doctors do not

*Source: "The Cure for all Diseases" by Hulder Regehr Clark

usually recommend this because of its dramatic effect, but it is one of the oldest folk remedies. Victorian children were subjected to high enemas, and up until the 1960's Women in childbirth were given enemas to make the job easier. East York General Hospital in Toronto STILL gives an enema when women go in to give birth.

I find colonics one of the quickest and most efficient ways to clear a cold or eliminate a long-standing illness. To facilitate the process, I generally take some calmag (calcium/magnesium) or Vitamin C tablets the evening before so that my lower bowel is clear, ready for the big flush! It's a simple procedure and takes around an hour. To find a colon therapist, look in the advertising section of your local Health and Wellness magazine, search the Internet, or ask at your local health store.

Another alternative is:

## The Salt Water Cleanse

Directions:
Add 2 level teaspoons of sea salt to one quart (or 2 pints) of warm water

Drink entire quart first thing in the morning on an empty stomach – it will wash through the entire tract in about an hour. The salt water has the same specific gravity as blood, so the kidneys cannot pick up the water and the blood cannot pick up the salt. If it doesn't work the first time, try adding more or less salt until you find a balance.

**The following cleanse is a fast and should only be undertaken for the full ten day period if you have already done the liver/gall bladder cleanse and/or had a colonic** (otherwise the first three days can be not very pleasant; headaches, nausea and tiredness).

The Grade B maple syrup in the cleanse contains a large variety of minerals and vitamins. These include: potassium, calcium, magnesium, manganese, iron, copper, phosphorus, sulphur, chlorine and silicon. Vitamin A, B1, B2, B6, C, nicotinic acid and pantothenic acid are also present.

# Master Cleanser

Use herbal laxative tea – last thing at night and first thing in the morning. During the fast, health conditions a person may have, but may not yet be aware of, show up as the body begins to release toxins. I find that the best thing about this cleanse is that after the first day or so you feel no hunger cravings as the body believes that it is being supplied with food by the Maple Syrup, which provides instant sugar and energy to the tissues.

The Master Cleanser can be safely done for up to forty days.
In fact it's an amazing way to clear the body of all bacteria and viruses.
Do not take vitamins or supplements while on this cleanse as this is a breaking down process, not a building up process.

## Master Cleanser[*]

**Two tbsp of lemon or lime juice (1/2 lemon)**

**2 tbsp of pure grade B maple syrup or type 'C' (from health store)**

**1/10 tsp cayenne pepper (red) or to taste**

**12 oz of purified water (warm or medium hot)**

Combine ingredients and drink. This will help to purify the liver.
You may fill several quart jars and drink all day long (six glasses is the recommended daily amount)

Do this for 3-10 Days
You can also drink mint tea if desired (for breath)

Fasting for 1-2 days a month on this drink can be very cleansing and rejuvenating.

*From the book: The Master Cleanser, by Stanley Burroughs.

**Fasting:**

- Dissolves and eliminates toxins and congestion from every part of the body
- Cleanses the kidneys and the digestive system
- Purifies the glands and cells
- Eliminates all unusable waste and hardened material in the joints and muscles
- Builds a healthy blood stream
- Relieves pressure and irritation in the nerves, arteries, and blood vessels
- Releases old low-energy emotions

An easier alternative to the Master Cleanser is a Juice Fast. You can basically drink any amount of fruit or vegetable juice for 3 days.
You still get the nutrients you need and your body will have a chance to heal itself and regenerate.

After all the cleaning out, it's time to add in the nutrients to replenish your body. Your body can absorb vitamins and minerals so much more easily after cleansing. Visit a nutritionist or natural health practitioner to build up your immune system. A recent study in the U.S. discovered that 90% of people surveyed had a nutritional deficiency. A study done at Rochester University (U.S.A) showed an iron deficiency in teen-age girls to be the cause of lower (below average) math results than boys in the same age group due to loss of iron through periods.

Having cleared your mental body by changing your thoughts and language patterns and your physical body by cleansing, it's time to address and clear the emotional body. Your physical body is simply a mirror of a combination of your past life belief system, your family or genetic system and your current core belief system. If something is not working well with that body, it is the final call for help from your unconscious asking for attention. Instead of wondering why someone got cancer, ask yourself why they gave it to themselves by not listening to earlier signals.

Louise Hay, the famous American author, studied the Chinese 'chi' energy system and the Japanese 'ki' system, which explains that the blockages in your electrical messaging system through incorrect thinking, incorrect eating or emotional repression eventually result in physical manifestation in the form of disease. She realized that in order to balance the energy and recover, we have to change our thinking patterns, core beliefs and eating and exercise habits.

Your body 'remembers' everything that has ever happened to it.  If you have ever watched a child being admonished, you will notice that the child's body becomes as small as possible in defence; the breath is held and the fear of the moment is then stored somewhere in the body, providing a temporary blockage in the natural energy flow.

Repeated verbal or physical punishment has a more lasting effect. The goal of any kind of therapy is to release these old patterns or blockages (which can be physical, emotional, mental or spiritual). You are the engineer of your health, just as you are the engineer of your own happiness, success and well-being.

Lack and limitation are defined by how many limiting beliefs (I'm not good enough, I'm not clever) and low-energy emotions (anger, sadness, guilt, shame, fear and anxiety) you may have stored in the unconscious mind.
I've found the best and easiest way to clear and release these permanently is with Time Line Therapy ™*, a method which takes you back to the root cause of the original event (and before the gestalt, or sequence of events that followed) to release the emotions, while preserving the learnings. By finding the root cause of the emotion or belief, clients complete enormous change in just one session.

Any low-energy word, low-energy thought, low-energy emotion or belief serves to interfere with and interrupt your access to love, joy and abundance. What also serves as an interruption to happiness is the belief that fear, anger, guilt, self-doubt and old limiting decisions are real. These emotions of the middle brain are a linear reality. When you open up to the idea that these old low-energy emotions do not really exist, but that they are simply names we give to feelings to describe an absence of  love and joy, you move towards life enhancing awareness and pure consciousness. You go from polarity to oneness. You allow yourself to gain power, passion, confidence and self-worth. You have more clarity, lucidity and understanding as you move towards your ultimate potential. Let's go on to give you some quick ways to clear some of the old stored emotions such as anger, fear, sadness and guilt.

The following story is a metaphor that your unconscious mind will under-

*Secret of Creating Your Future – Tad James

stand, even though some of the language is unusual by normal standards.

Record yourself speaking aloud as you read the following script using a cassette recorder/ karaoke machine:

# *Goodbye to Negative Emotions and Old Beliefs**

*You may want to just settle back and allow yourself to relax only as quickly as your conscious mind will allow you. Perhaps you can make yourself more comfortable as you begin to bring your attention to your breathing now.*
*I'm wondering if you feel some fluttering in the eyelids, or the cheeks flushing, or one hand may feel different from the other as you relax more deeply.*
*With every breath, with every beat of your heart you may.... **just let go now.***
*Breathing deeply – and that deep breathing increases the rate of your metabolism, enriching the body with oxygen as you begin to feel lighter and lighter now, awakening the senses as you begin to search for the answer inside…the body.*
*Will you **feel the shift deep inside now** …or upon awakening?*
*Searching, surrendering to that great wisdom inside yourself as you find yourself remembering now. What is the question you need to ask that will allow you to move into joy now or in the next few minutes?*
*Back over the years, over the months – smaller and smaller 9, 8, 7, 6, 5, 4, 3 months and fully formed, 7 weeks and you have a heartbeat. As you remember now becoming smaller and lighter, smaller and lighter, remembering back to when you used to breathe liquid and were fed through a cord attached to your abdomen. Feeling connected… to an ocean of inner knowledge.*
*And find yourself now… as you go deeper and deeper inside to the source, to the quantum space between the cells which is pure light… becoming lighter and lighter, floating back to the dawn of existence.*
*Remember… remember… remember… the dawn.*
*Swirling clouds on a mountainside evaporate into morning mist and then the mist clears to reveal a trickle of water as it makes its way down over rocks and pebbles, sparkling, reflecting the light as it laughs and sings its way through soft new greenery.*
*Floating above, you may catch a current of warm air and find that you can fly and soar like an eagle, above the earth, above the ageless scene beneath you. Follow the path of the water downwards… and as your awareness increases you may notice that the weather is changing. Storm clouds form above the earth. The*

*All scripts in this book are available on CD (with background music) from: www.hypnonow.com

*sky darkens. You may want to fly above the clouds where it is still… and light as you watch the lightning and the angry, powerful energy of the storm beneath. Thunder cracks across the earth and a flash of light illuminates a small animal, shivering and cowering in the depths of the forest. Water pours down from the sky, turning the brook into a stream.*

*From your viewpoint, gliding and soaring, you can observe the storm subsiding and the sky clearing now. Sunlight dances off the water droplets on the newly cleansed earth beneath. You observe the small animal scampering away, having survived the storm, damp but free now to get on with its life.*

*The stream becomes stronger as it follows its path ever down towards the sea, joining with more streams until it becomes a powerful river.*

*Forging its way along, moulding the earth into a deep channel, the river becomes a torrent of surging power. You may hear the rushing of the river as it flows over the earth faster and faster, becoming a waterfall pounding onto the rocks below, smoothing those rocks with an endless, powerful force, then spreading out and flooding the valley.*

*Glide higher on a current of air and witness the most magical scene as the waterfall becomes a lake, calm and peaceful, glinting in the sunshine. The day warms the air gently. A softness, a haze envelopes the scene beneath.*

*Lazy, seemingly endless moments of relaxation and harmony, as time slows down for you now. Swoop down and taste an endless supply of cool refreshing water as your body and spirit drink the clear liquid of life.*

*Regretfully, the water spreads out and makes its way sadly down through the trees that stand below the lake. The water is the source of their strength. As you fly above, you may lose sight of the water for a while, as it seems to disappear beneath the canopy of trees below. You may wonder if it's gone because sometimes you can't see beneath the surface, but part of you knows that it's still there, making its way underneath the earth, sometimes out of sight for a long time.*

*It may even seem that the water is completely gone, as the parched earth dries in the heat of the summer sun, but the water has simply travelled deeper. It seems that the joy of life is hiding beneath the surface, but secretly the water has simply headed downwards to the protection of the cool earth.*

*Continuing the journey to the sea, the water appears again, first forming tiny rivulets, then streams, then again into a sparkling river making its way easily around obstacles as it gathers strength, surging and powering as every stone and rock in its way gets swept aside by its power and might.*

*It slows down as the ground becomes more flat, winds and meanders, finally* meeting the sea, the ocean, where it will dance for a while and then evaporate into clouds to begin the journey again.

You may even think that you can... remember the sound of the waves rolling against the shore.

And how wonderful it would be to swim in the azure sea, above a living breathing coral reef. You may want to dive beneath the surface – deep below to observe that sunlight dappling on the coral beneath, observing colourful fish darting and dancing in and out of the living coral. The ocean is made up of the same 96 elements that make up your body now. Remember back to living and breathing that water. Programmed from within, moving forward in a self-contained ongoing process of growth and development. You know the answer – you always did.

Perhaps you can find yourself in a current of warm water. Swim upwards now with the warm stream towards the surface, pushing and floating towards the light. What's the very first thing...the very first thing?

As you break free now, take a deep breath. Feel yourself becoming lighter and lighter, floating up into the air, letting go of old beliefs. It's easy to let go of all those old beliefs and decisions. You do it every day. When you were seven you believed you were seven. You had a birthday and believed you were eight, letting go of the idea that you were seven. Yesterday you believed that today was tomorrow. Tomorrow you'll believe that today is yesterday. Life is all about correcting outdated thoughts and ...changing your mind.

The gentle sunlight warms your face and a light breeze plays with your body as you feel a surge of joy. It's time to make a new decision now to let go of any low-energy emotions that don't support your awesome magnificence.

You may want to think of the most ecstatic moment of your life – the visible and invisible becoming one. One moment when... you feel totally happy now. Every cell now remembering and reconnecting......(pause).

Every time you look up you can instantly connect with the feeling of freedom that this memory brings. Remembering the soaring of the eagle with its power and might as it flies upwards, always seeing near and far in clear perspective.

As I count backwards from five to one you can return to the body with a new certainty that you are at the beginning of a new journey to a future full of hope and light, truth and joy.

Five... tingling and thrilling to be here again

Four...loving the new you

Three ... clean and light, full of life and health

*Two…be free, to be me, to be happy*
*One… Open your eyes to the dawn of a brand new day*

\*\*\*\*\*\*\*\*\*\*\*\*\*\*\*\*\*\*\*\*\*\*\*\*\*\*\*\*\*\*\*\*\*\*\*\*\*\*\*\*\*\*\*\*\*\*\*\*\*\*\*\*\*\*\*\*\*\*\*\*\*\*\*\*

This metaphor will begin to loosen up your model of the world, making it easier for your natural state of joy to emerge. It's good to listen to it at night just before sleep, or in the morning just after awakening, as your inner and outer minds are more aligned at these times.

## *Control, or Control Issues?*

By viewing events more objectively, you regain control of your life. Being in control means that you can make better choices. Are you in control of your life in every area? Do you feel that you are aware of and using all your potential? If not, you may find that some low-energy emotions and events begin to arrive in your life, as your unconscious mind tries to draw your attention to the fact that something is not balanced. At this point, being in control may be replaced by control issues; the inappropriate need to control people or events outside of oneself due to the absence of real control. Life management may then be replaced with a need to have perfection or be perfect as the person tries to keep ahead of the surfacing feelings of discomfort.

The names we've given to the main feelings of discomfort are: anger, fear, sadness/depression and guilt. Let's go ahead and clear these low-energy feelings one by one in order to regain the feeling of being in charge of and creating your life, because you can then access higher consciousness feelings of empowerment.

## *Clear the Anger*

Anger is a wonderful emotional energy which can be used to stimulate action. Many great changes in society have been made by someone getting angry enough to make a difference. The opposite emotion to anger is passion, which is the best direction to channel anger if it does come up to the surface. Anger is an emotion that is often due to unrealistic and unfulfilled entitlement or expectations. It's a need for control or power. The energy becomes inappropriate when it is internalized without being released productively or constructively.

Anger is mainly found where boundaries have been crossed (imaginary or otherwise). It can also be found when childhood situations are repeated, as your unconscious mind tries to bring to the surface any unresolved issues in order to clear away old emotional baggage.

There are two types of anger which we need to address. The first is situational anger or anger due to circumstances, such as when someone treads on your toe, or you find that the person you came to visit isn't in. This is called externalized anger.

The other type of anger goes deeper. This is the internalized anger. It's the slow burn which is felt and may pop up at any time, due to issues originating in childhood (or before). This anger is something which needs to be addressed by a professional. Again, Time Line Therapy ™ and Hypnotherapy are the fastest tools available for this anger release.

How do you release anger if it does come up? One of the easiest ways if you haven't got a therapist within reach is to do physical exercise of any kind. The workout preferably needs to make you breathe heavily, so sex is as good an exercise as running! Physical exercise allows you to take the energy and channel it into something productive.

Another way is to increase and free the energy attached to the emotion by using a sounding technique. Ideally this would be in a place away from other people as this exercise is very loud!

Whenever you are in the car, or in the bath or shower, choose a word which resonates with you – anger, fear, guilt, shame, sadness, or a high-energy word – love, peace, calm, joy, happy, passion, power. Take your attention to your Chi Gung (three finger widths below your belly button) or power centre, take a deep breath and call or sing the word as loud and long as you can.
The emphasis is on the vowel sound, so the word 'fear' being a vowel diagraph would sound like: feeeee….eeeee…..aaaaaaaaaaarrrr!
Continue the vowel sound for at least a minute, until you can feel the muscles in your Chi Gung area go tight and your face is red! The sound eeeee, by the way, opens the heart centre and aaaaaa opens the third eye energy which increases intuition and manifestation.

You can sound someone's name or call out meeeeeeeeeeeee! as loud as you like. Freeeeeeeeeeeeeeeeeeeeeeeeee. The longer and more intense the vowel sound is, the quicker you feel great!

By the time you get to the quiet space at the end of the noise you've made, you've eliminated any unwanted emotion by changing the frequency of the sound attached to it and cleared the way for a pleasant emotion to take its place. I've had some funny looks from people when I've been doing this at a traffic stop, so find a place where you can make noise alone!

The reason that this exercise works was proven in a Japanese university. They developed a method for erasing sound by using the sound of an opposing frequency. Sounds of opposite frequency cannot resonate. In fact, by creating the exact opposite noise, researchers can eliminate the original sound.

An interesting variation of this exercise is to choose a part of your body that doesn't feel great and imagine what word would be there if you have to choose a word or feeling. Sound that word, and then find what word is underneath it. Keep going until you recover a high-energy word like 'love' or 'safe'. Sound that word and you'll feel wonderful. Guaranteed.
This is also a great method for releasing physical pain from the body.

Obviously, the real key is to prevent anger by staying relaxed and aware of any situation that would induce a feeling of lack of control or intrusion into your space. Also remember to remove the word 'anger' from your language patterns. Switch to 'strong emotion'.

**Some Other Solutions to Clearing Anger**

Fresh fruits/vegetables
Cleansing
Exercise – aerobic, or alpha stimulating such as yoga or swimming
Singing
Deep breathing
High-energy Thinking and Speaking
Meditation and Self Hypnosis

**For Deeper Anger release**
Outside therapy (Time Line or Hypnosis) for internalized anger to find root cause.

# *Fear*
### (False Evidence Appearing Real)*

Fear is simply the absence of trust. So…are you happy, healthy, loved, prosperous, adventurous, confident, and comfortable in your environment and home? If not, do you trust that you are heading in that direction? Or are you living in fear?  Because it is fear which is not allowing you to have all of those wonderful things.

The need to be in control inappropriately is either fear-based or anger-based. If anger is a feeling of not being in control, fear is a feeling that you are being controlled by someone or something outside of yourself, which is not actually possible! I hear about people who think they are 'possessed' and my response is: Why did they allow themselves to get possessed by someone or something? It's a great distraction technique for not being accountable!

There are currently 20,000,000 websites on the Internet devoted to fears and phobias. The only thing to really be afraid of is standing still for too long, or of fear itself. Fear is a primary survival response which was very useful in the past when we had to take action by fighting or fleeing from predators, as fear increases alertness. The hormones produced by a fear response are mainly adrenaline and cortisol, which produce physical sensations of dry mouth, increased heart and respiration rate, insomnia, increased blood pressure and a sensation of fluttering in the stomach area. When the fear is over, a sense of release or euphoria is experienced. These days we even induce fear for fun just to get the high resulting from a fear response! It's great in small doses – just go on a roller coaster ride, bungee-jump, or go white-water rafting! Your alertness is increased and you feel more alive.

The modern day fears of not having enough, being enough or doing enough are more abstract and bring the same physiological response, without the subsequent release. Action is needed, just as it was needed in the past, to bring fulfillment and meaning to your life.

*Through the Open Door- Secrets of Self-Hypnosis by Kevin Hogan/Mary Lee La Bay

Ask yourself: "What am I afraid of most: not having enough, not being enough, or not doing enough?" Then ask: "What is it that I don't have/ am not being or am not doing?" It's useful to write the answer so that you can more easily find a solution and take action.

Fear and judgement create separation. The clearing of fear creates enormous inner resources and psychological strength. When abundance and trust is present in every area of your life, then fear is absent. It's not usual to wake up in the morning and feel concerned about whether there is enough air for you to breathe all day. You just take it for granted. There is enough for us all and more. So how do you feel about having an abundance of love, money, and health?

Are you really ready for it all?

**It's time to make changes**

The universe is an ever unfolding flower which changes second by second. Make those changes. Change what you normally have for breakfast. Change your routine. Decide to change your job, your home, improve your relation-ships. Don't feel comfortable changing one of these? Then change everything else except the thing you most need to change and then that last one will change automatically! The key to clearing fear is decision-making and forward-moving action.

## *Clear the Fear*

Before we look at fear release, you might want to find a safe place to have as a retreat if you feel at any time less than comfortable. Your unconscious mind knows what it needs to do to let go of any stored low-energy emotions and will not allow you to experience something you are not ready to process. However, it is sometimes good to have a 'safe spot' as a backup.

Imagine your dream relaxation holiday. It might be a beach, a forest glade, a mountain, a wood with a stream running through it, a temple. Anywhere in fact, that you would feel totally safe. Close your eyes and for two minutes imagine as vividly as you can that you are in your safe spot. Can you feel the water? Smell the air? Feel the sun on your face, the breeze in your hair? What can you hear? What taste is in your mouth? Paint your safe place as colourfully as you can.

Now, imagine the sun pouring from the sky into the top of your head and stretch lazily. If you wish you can erect a fence or a forest around your safe place.

# Release the Fear – Free your Future

## Open to the Joy

Much fear is inherited fear, or fear that we picked up from our parents' fears during the imprinting phase, the first seven years of childhood, so it's important that we recognize and release not only what we think of as our own fears, but also the fears we took on without realizing.

Sit comfortably for this exercise. Play some quiet music, or stay in silence, close your eyes and relax.

**Transform the fear**

Imagine that you are in a private room. There is a door to your right and a window to your left. Outside is a beautiful day. The sun is shining and you can see through the window into a park or gardens.

Observe the door opening. Imagine your mother's biggest fear coming in. What would it look like if you imagine it as a person or thing? Observe the person or thing move to the side of your bed. Say "Hello". How do you feel about her/him/it? What is her/his/its name? Make up a name if you can't immediately think of one. Can you find it in yourself to feel sorry for the person or thing, knowing the kind of life they had? What can you do to the fear to make her/him/it beautiful? Ask what he/she or it needs from you to help. Use your imagination to do anything you can do to make the person or thing friendly or comfortable.

**Some suggestions:**
    Use a magic wand
    Take her/him/it into the sunlight

Make the person or thing smaller so that you can cuddle her/him to make her/him/it feel better

Get a nurse, angel or visitor to come in to help you.

Give her/him/it a gift.

Help her/him/it step out of their 'skin' to find out if there's someone nice underneath.

Touch her/him/it softly and tell them that you care.

After the person or thing feels better, take them to the door or open window and set them free (watch her/him/it disappear, change into a butterfly, walk out).

Repeat the exercise for your father's fear and then repeat it again for your own fear. Remember to retreat to your 'safe place' if you need to, for just a second or two, then go back to the exercise.

**Exercise to Feel Safe**

This exercise can be done anywhere. The key to its success is to change your physiology. Make sure that your back is straight up and your head is erect, your chin tilted slightly upward (imagine a piece of elastic pulling the top of your head).

*Imagine above you the most beautiful sun – a disc of yellow-energy. Breathe in the sun to the count of eight. Hold the energy in the centre of your chest to the count of eleven, then release it slowly. As you release, imagine yourself surrounded by a beautiful protective bubble of radiant energy. You might want to pray or feel thankful to raise your vibration higher.*

*Breathe the light in again and imagine yourself in the most beautiful place you can think of. Remember a time when you felt really safe. It could be a childhood memory, a new love, a recent promotion. Find every instance of happiness and safety in your memory bank and when you find one that makes you feel good, stay with it. Remember how wonderful that moment feels.*

*Where are you holding that memory in your physical body? If you don't know, where in your body would it be if you had to choose a place? Continue the breathing until your heartbeat and breathing rate slow down.*

Fear of failure is not the only fear people have. People can be just as afraid of success, due to old ideas or limiting beliefs about it. Love, money, health, comfort and purpose are your reward and your right.

When I was 28, I decided that I wanted to work in Rome, Italy. I had applied for teaching jobs but had had no success because typically the schools were not prepared to pay someone's fare on the off-chance that the applicant may be suitable. I decided to go for a ten day holiday. I figured that the least good thing that could happen was that I wouldn't speak to anyone and I would come back with a suntan, so I packed a few books and off I went. It was magic! The first day I met a lady who knew of an American woman in her sixties, who was happy for the extra money from renting out a spare bedroom, which meant that my resources were able to be stretched further. The American, Jane, was lovely. She introduced me to her daughter Simonetta, who had worked in England and spoke English. She in turn told me about teaching jobs being advertised in the Rome Herald Tribune. I was offered three jobs, took the best, went home to pack and lived in Italy for the next three years. An amazing experience.

All of my friends said "Oh my God! You are so brave! What if you didn't like it? What if… What if…?" My reply?
"England is an hour away by air – if I don't like it I can come back!"

Find the courage inside you to change. Do anything different – especially things that are 'not you'. If being 'you' hasn't made you happy so far, having a go at new things must be worth it! Sitting on the fence is not a pleasant place to stay for very long because the universe will find a way to change you sooner or later. Your body will also give you a big clue to if you are not balanced for any length of time. Your dis-ease will result in just that…disease.
One of the most common emotional dis-eases this century has been depression.

# *Depression*

Depression is an external trigger related to a sense of loss. It's about not feeling that you have permission to express yourself and possibly unresolved anger. It has come to mean disappointment, as in "I'm depressed that I didn't get what I wanted for my birthday." It's a natural phenomenon which happens when someone is consciously feeling overwhelmed. As a temporary external condition, it's useful in that it allows someone to take time off from feelings in order to bring emotions back into balance by making the person feel that they need to take time out to do …nothing. A quick solution for feeling down is just do exactly that. Watch a DVD or read a book. Pray. Give your spirit a rest.

Someone who is deeply depressed for any length of time needs a support system from an external source, such as friends or a therapist who will work with them to help them become more objective. New information coming in, in the form of a night out or a new course of learning, is a good way to distract the person from the depression, with Time Line Therapy ™ and/or Hypnosis again my therapies of choice for finding and clearing root cause.

Stress or depression uses up light stored inside the cells of the body to help us to cope*. Light is stored in the body by the DNA in the form of photons. Stress, illness and depression increase the rate of biophoton emissions as a defence mechanism designed to bring the individual's energy back into balance.

Ideally, the healthiest body would be glowing with light - the nearest state possible to God. Clairvoyantly, when I see a healthy aura, it looks like the person is surrounded by light. Someone who is not healthy, or who is depressed or on drugs, appears to be sitting in a grey (or even black) cloud. I was surprised once to see a man who was a drug addict with a ring of darkness almost half a metre thick surrounding his body. In other words, he had used up his supply of light from the body and was not at all well as there was no more light for his cells to use to communicate with one another.

How do we get more light? By excellent nutrition (the fuel the body uses to convert to energy), particularly any fruit or vegetable that's fresh and raw, and by excellent thinking patterns and actions.

To release old low-energy emotions consciously if you ever feel down, plan to cry one evening. Make sure you can be alone, and time it! So, for example, you may decide: "I am going to cry between nine o'clock and eleven o'clock tonight." (Two hours is a good period of time to allow).

Also by getting the conscious mind involved and engaged again you gain objectivity which will begin to release the depression.

Find all the sad CDs or cassettes you can, or get ready to replay all the sad

*Fritz Alfred Popp –University of Marburg (Germany)

scenes from a movie that you know will help you to cry and get them set up. At nine o'clock exactly press the play button and really, really feel sorry for yourself. Then concentrate on finding understanding and compassion for yourself. You have innate integrity and an ability to discover your own unique truth about your life. Allow yourself the grace of grieving as you would allow someone else. By validating unhappiness and intensifying it, you let it go. I've never managed to cry the whole two hours when I do this. I run out of things to think about long before that time and I reward myself with a good book or a glass of wine.

The time limit is the most important element in this exercise. Giving yourself a time limit sets a boundary line and gives permission to the unconscious mind for quick release of the emotions. If you still don't feel better after this, then seek professional help, as the depression may be more deep rooted.

## Guilt and Shame

Guilt is one of the most unpleasant emotions to carry around. It comes from the Anglo- Saxon word 'gylt' for sin or crime. It's really nature's way of giving us a conscience. Guilt is the word we use for the low-energy emotion that people feel when they've disappointed others. Shame is the feeling that comes when they are disappointed with themselves. Guilt, shame, resentment and sadness are the emotions which are most draining of one's energy and resources. Low-energy thoughts and lowered immune system may result from harbouring any of these low frequency feelings for any length of time (longer than two minutes!).

Recent research indicates that long term unresolved resentment is a clear way to get cancer because as long as people see themselves as victims, the guilt that is projected has to return as punishment; particularly guilt held on an unconscious level. Any unresolved issue will eventually show up in the body.

### 'What the mind suppresses, the body expresses'

Holding a grievance or grudge separates people from themselves and separates them from truth and joy. This separation leads to outward projection, resulting in imbalance. In reality, not forgiving others means that self-forgiveness and acceptance is absent (as without, so within).

Telling someone to just get over it is not very effective, so how can you let go? The Hawaiian people have a wonderful exercise that they do for release and forgiveness. They call it Ho'o Pono Pono. The following is an adaptation of this process:

## Open up Your Heart -Forgiveness and Release

**Record the following script in your own voice onto a cassette tape and** listen to it every day until you feel your energy start to return, along with a wonderful feeling of freedom. You'll be amazed at the results.

*The more you breathe, the more you relax.*
*Imagine now, a magical forest, a beautiful safe place in nature. It's a lovely day. The sun is dappling through the trees, the birds are singing sweetly and you can hear the sound of water trickling over the rocks and pebbles from a nearby stream. You may smell cedar, pine or damp earth.*
*In a clearing, find a comfortable place at the base of a strong oak tree, sit down and just experience this feeling of tranquility and harmony, as you absorb all the knowledge and wisdom ... from this great tree of the forest. You ...feel a sense of peace and safety as the sunlight dapples through the trees.*
*Perhaps you can hear the leaves rustle as they play with the breeze. They seem to be giving you a message from your unconscious...mind to ......just let go. Your conscious mind can listen now, or simply continue observing the sounds and sights of nature.*
*You may observe the wooden bridge that is over the water. Raise your eyes to the bluest of blue skies... a sky which seems to go on forever.... Take a deep breath and allow yourself to let go..o..o..o..*
*A shaft of sunlight which warms and softens your face slowly relaxes your whole body. As the cells, nerves, tissues and organs absorb this wonderful, light, breathe deeply and slowly, relaxing further with every breath. The sunlight makes its way automatically over your scalp, relaxing your head and neck.*
*Find your shoulders relaxing as you feel the light warming, relaxing and releasing all the muscles and tissues. The light moves down your spine, strengthening and releasing as it goes, rippling and relaxing. Feel a new suppleness in the muscles and nerves surrounding every vertebra.*
*As the warm, powerful, compelling light flows down though your body, feel every organ- your heart, liver, lungs, stomach- relax and free itself, moving in perfect harmony with the rest of the body.*

*Your arms and hands relax as the light enters every cell, renewing and revitalizing as it goes. You may feel a tingling sensation in your right or left hand- whichever hand this is for you- which shows you that you are relaxing even further. Your buttocks, hips and genitals relax as the light moves downwards over and through your body. You may notice a sensation of heaviness in your thighs, knees and calves as you relax even further now.*

*In this comfortable place of safety, you suddenly notice a wonderful angel, standing to your left, who holds a laser sword of light. Observe the angel's presence of unconditional love and allow yourself to be bathed in the golden glow of acceptance.*

*Now imagine some people standing across the other side of the bridge, in a circular area, surrounded by trees. These are all the people you know this life time who have an emotional tie to you. You may see people there whom you haven't thought of in years.*

*Observe a person come towards you over the bridge and* **walk forward to meet this person***... in the centre of your clearing. Notice that the person looks a little different from the way you remember, because this is the person's higher self, dressed in flowing, beautiful robes.*

*You suddenly feel a cord attaching this person to your body. Where is the cord attached? (pause)... Where is the cord attached to their body? (pause)*

*Listen to this person ask your forgiveness for whatever he or she did to you, knowingly or unknowingly, this lifetime or any other. As you sense that the life they lived was not easy, do you* **understand now** *why that person behaved the way they did? Can you feel softened?*

*It's now time to ask her or him for forgiveness for whatever you did, knowingly or unknowingly, this lifetime or any other.*

*When you have both come now to an understanding, ask the angel to cut the cord with the laser of light. Take a deep breath, hold it and ...***get ready to release** *......the breath... by saying the word "Now!" aloud when...* **you are ready** *(pause).*

*As the laser cuts the cord, breathe a deep breath and feel the sensation of release and empowerment. Watch the cord turn into pure light and be re-absorbed by both yourself and the other person.*

*Feel how much stronger you are now. Observe the other person smile at you gratefully and stand a little taller. Watch as he or she leaves the clearing, goes back over the bridge with a spring in their step and disappears into the forest.*

*Get ready to let go of the next person, who is walking towards you. As the person stands in front of you, observe where the cord is attached to your body and to her/his body. Listen to this person ask your forgiveness for whatever he or she did* to you, knowingly or unknowingly, this lifetime or any other (pause).

As you sense that the life they lived was not easy, do you …**understand now** …why that person behaved the way they did? Can you feel softened?

It's time to ask her or him for forgiveness for whatever you did, knowingly or unknowingly, this lifetime or any other.

When you have both… **come now to an understanding,** …ask the angel to cut the cord with the laser of light. Take a deep breath, hold it and …**get ready to release** ……the breath… by saying the word "Now!" aloud when… **you are ready**. As the laser cuts the cord, breathe a deep breath and feel a wonderful sensation of release and empowerment. Watch the cord turn into pure light and be re-absorbed by both yourself and the other person.

Feel how much stronger you are now. Observe the other person smile at you grate-fully and stand a little taller. Watch as he or she leaves the clearing, goes back over the bridge with a spring in their step and disappears into the forest.

You'll notice a group of people coming towards you from the other side of the bridge, excitedly smiling with anticipation at the thought of approaching freedom. As they gather in the … **clearing before you , the path is open** to new ways and endless possibilities for the future.

Notice the cords attaching you to the group and the group to you. You may see a number of cords attached to different parts of your body. How thick or thin are the cords?

Listen to all these people ask your forgiveness for whatever they did to you, knowingly or unknowingly, this lifetime or any other. As you sense that the life they lived was not easy, do you …**understand now** …why they behaved the way they did?

Can you … **feel softened by the knowledge…?**

It's time now to ask their forgiveness for whatever you did, knowingly or unknow-ingly, this lifetime or any other.

When you have **come to an understanding,** ask the angel to cut the cords with the laser of light. Take a deep breath, hold it and …**get ready to release** ……the breath… by saying the word "Now!" aloud when… **you are ready.** (pause)

As the laser cuts the cord, breathe a deep breath ……**feel** the sensation of release and empowerment. Watch the cords turn into the pure light of joy and be re-absorbed by both yourself and the people, into the solar plexus.

Feel how much stronger you are now. Observe everyone smile at you gratefully and stand a little taller. Watch as they leave the clearing and go back over the bridge with a spring in their step. They are laughing, waving and talking as they disappear into the forest.

*The angel puts down the laser of light and embraces you.*
*Feel the approval and unconditional love of the angel, take a deep breath and* **become aware of a new sensation in your body.**
*It's a feeling that* **you know you accept and forgive others.** *You know* **you forgive and accept yourself,** *fully and completely, now.*

As you learn to accept others and appreciate them for their courage, you may recognize that people are not their behaviours. Truly look for the five year old in everyone and you'll observe their light and beauty inside. Your ability to connect and communicate with other people will increase your aptitude to achieve intimacy, understanding and trust.

# THE FIFTH KEY –
## The Power of COMMUNICATION

Communication is the most important key to effect understanding and trust. It bonds humanity together. Let's start by looking back into the past to observe just how far we've already come:

## *Where did Communication Begin?*

The use of gestures and body language, many researchers believe, began at least 4 million years ago when bi-pedalism, a characteristic of the hominid line, freed up the hands, enabling expressive communication. Most hominid fossils, dating back from 4,000,000 to less than 2,000,000 years ago, have been found on the east side of the Rift Valley in Africa. The apes that became Hominids were largely confined to the east of the valley, where forest gave way to open savannah, the territory of the ancestors of lions and hyenas. This made the hominids vulnerable to attack.

Evidence of groups and socialization also appears around this time, possibly as a means of protection. Non-verbal communication could have been established as a result of this more cohesive and co-operative social structure, one of the benefits of which is silence, a great protective device around predators. Intentional non-verbal communication such as pointing, the indication of spatial awareness, is not found in other primates and is the one single thing that separates us from other species. In fact, human babies point automatically at a very early age.

Primates are largely visual. Vision is much more highly developed in both monkeys and people. Monkeys, chimps and gorillas have been taught several hundred hand signals to indicate expressive, voluntary communication. The same area of the brain that is activated during hand gestures (the lower left lobe of the brain – Broca's area) is the same area that is activated during speech, leading to a possible conclusion that gestures were the forerunner of the speech system.

The brain has three major parts: the reptilian brain, the middle or limbic brain, and the most recently developed part of the brain, the cerebral cortex. The ancient reptilian brain's focus is physical movement and survival.
The middle brain links mainly with our emotions – fear, anger, love, affection, and also to communication. It's called the family brain, or the limbic brain. This is the group brain system that began to evolve as we began to socialize. Its goals are short term and focused on good / bad, right / wrong, yours / mine. It's habitual, hierarchical and simplistic. It does not have a capacity to visualize or grow because it thinks in terms of polarities.

The newest part of the brain is the cerebral cortex. New is relative, of course! It has only developed in the last 150 -200,000 years and it is here that language began in the form of gestures. What is amazing is that studies done at the University of Chicago show that gestures take on a grammatical role if people are prevented from speaking. In the North Central Desert of Australia, gestures form a very intricate and grammatically accurate living language for women observing speech taboos following the death of a close relative.

Sign language used by the Plains Indians of North America served mainly as a means of communication between tribes who spoke different languages.
Sign language for the deaf has only been accepted as a language since the late 1950's and again it has all the characteristics, including grammatical rules, of a true language.

Essential to language is the ability to understand and take on the mental perspective of others. "Mirror" neurons are active when a monkey or human is watching someone's actions, possibly the beginning of the ability to mirror someone's actions or speech to gain rapport. We still use gestures and body language to supplement speech; in fact we use body language for around 55% of all communication. Just ask someone to describe what a spiral looks like using words!

Complex language as we know it only emerged around 65,000 years ago. Its origin could explain why Homo sapiens came to dominate over the Neanderthals of Europe or Homo Erectus of South East Asia. Why is that? Because the one amazing property of speech that makes it different from any other form of communication is its ability to be generative. We can now think back into the past and forward into the future. We can fantasize and imagine beyond and outside of space and time, giving us endless possibilities that can be conveyed with just a single word!

Speech is so important because it sets us apart from every other species. However the language that we use now still has words that were formulated 65,000 years ago to describe the feelings and emotions that were emerging from the middle brain's polarity thinking. By consciously changing our language  we can consciously create a different, more open and happy world for ourselves.

The neocortex is the most recent part of the brain to develop. Neocortical inputs are mainly from the frontal lobe, which modulates initiative, imagination and social awareness. This higher brain function is where your magic formula for happiness begins, as you connect with the higher consciousness. Use of the higher brain produces consistent success in your everyday life. You can now plan your goals and visualize wonderful possibilities with this magical tool. Rather than use the higher brain, or cerebral cortex, as a means to rescue you when you feel less than happy, it's time to learn to utilize it and live in it by spring-cleaning your language of antiquated middle brain polarity thought processes; going beyond what you think you want to find out what you really need. It's a whole new language, a whole new way.

By clearing the interference pattern, which acts rather like static, of past low-energy emotions and limiting beliefs (or what is not), you increase your ability to manifest your desires because it allows you to access the higher brain directly. The creative integration of the recently developed cerebral cortex with the older limbic brain allows you to tap into the whole system.

How do you know if you're using the higher brain to guide your life? Test it by consciously spending half an hour to an hour every day in solitude and just listen to your thoughts. The Dalai Lama advises: "Spend some time alone every day." The best time of day to do this is last thing at night or first thing in the morning. Listening to your own voice shows you what your unconscious mind is busy thinking about. I've found that the more I love life and myself, the more I hear my inner voice simply singing or giving me encouragement inside my head. The more I expect wonderful things to happen, the more they do.

As you clear the interference patterns from your mind, the higher consciousness in the cerebral cortex begins to develop further and you will experience a sense of inner peace and trust, even when things are not going as well as you'd like. In fact, things move through your life much more quickly as you leap to higher levels.

You will find that you are then always in a state of confidence, feeling empowered, in control and self-motivated. Concepts quickly become reality as you take action to make life happen. You love who and where you are in your life and you are hopeful for the progress of humanity.

## *The Language of Rapport*

What is rapport exactly? The dictionary definition is: "Relation of mutual understanding, or trust and agreement between people."

**Why do I need to know how to build rapport? What will it do for me exactly?**

- ❖ It increases your sense of self confidence and charisma
- ❖ You can immediately make a great first impression in both personal and professional situations
- ❖ You'll send the right signals and become more interesting to other people
- ❖ You'll understand other people more easily and appreciate their model of the world
- ❖ Your attitude will change as you use your skills to become more welcoming and enthusiastic
- ❖ You'll increase intimacy levels in all your relationships

Important as language is, only 7% of communication is verbal. The other 93% is communicated unconsciously through body language (55%) and tone (38%).*

These secret language signals are often sent out and interpreted without your conscious knowledge, as your unconscious mind commands this whole area of

*Robert Birdwhistle, 1970 – Pennsylvania University

communication. At Harvard University, psychologists found that the attitude that students formed towards new teachers in the first two seconds remained the same throughout the course!

This is your chance to develop rapport at a conscious and unconscious level, enabling you to initiate the building of a lasting rapport in 90 seconds or less. Is that possible? Of course! Babies do it without the use of either language or tone. They instinctively match and mirror anyone who cares to put their face close – smiles are exchanged, eye contact is established, touch is returned as baby squeezes your finger. A baby's very survival depends on people wanting to spend time with it. The "Aaaah" appeal of a baby is no coincidence. Even before birth the foetus matches the body rhythms and functions of the mother.

Studies show that eye contact during the first three months of life establishes the ability of an adult to achieve emotional intimacy. Babies who do not get close physical contact or eye contact; for instance, those babies who are born pre-term and are put in an incubator, or babies who have a mother with few maternal instincts, will not find it easy in later life to establish close relationships or respond to intimacy. It's instinctive for children to mimic, particularly during the first seven years: the 'imprint' phase, when copying is a natural way for a child to learn about the world and relationships.

It's up to us, as adults, to think carefully of the effect our words and actions may have on children. As an example, a study in California of toddlers, who each wore a tape recorder for a week, showed that whenever they were communicating with adults about anything, 85% of the time they were told "No!"

Some of us had good role models in the form of a parent who is a great communicator. My mother can walk into a room full of strangers and immediately feel comfortable and make herself liked. I too find it very easy to meet people and make myself at home. Matching or mirroring the other person's body language is one of the easiest ways to make someone feel that you like them. Another way is to hold your head slightly to one side, nodding. This tells the other person that you like them and also shows that you are allowing them to lead.

However, children who have parents with few communication skills, or children who have emotional interference patterns (which tend to lead to the child dissociating) may find themselves 'mismatching' without realizing. The other person feels uncomfortable around the mismatcher without knowing why and probably will avoid them in the future, confirming the mismatcher's belief that somehow they are not likeable. Their rhythms just don't match those of other people, so it may appear that the other person doesn't like them.

The more you are similar to other people the more they will like you. In fact, it's automatic when you meet someone new to establish common ground. You ask questions about their life, looking for something you can talk about together. When you find that something, the relationship takes a comfortable step forward. If you do not find commonality, you quickly move on.

The simple fact is that people like people who are like themselves.

We use our five senses to experience the world, through sight, hearing, touching, smelling or tasting. The four main systems we use to audit the information we receive are visual, auditory, kinaesthetic and auditory digital (self-talk) and we all have one which tends to be more dominant. Visually dominant people make up around 60% of the population. People who are primarily visual have an advantage over auditory or kinaesthetic people, both from the perspective of their ability to observe and copy postures, movements and signals more easily and also the fact that they tend to use eye contact more easily, making them appear to be friendlier.

If you are not as comfortable around other people as you would like, you can learn to increase your sensory acuity using integrity and respect for others to create warm responses. You can learn the following rules and apply them with guaranteed success. Fake it until you make it and then get ready to let go and let flow!

## Like me! Like me!

We all seek approval – from our parents, our friends, peers and ourselves. Whether we know it or not, we instinctively want to be liked. You have less than 10 seconds to make that lasting first impression when you meet someone new. Your job is to reassure the other person short term that you are safe to be around and then work on longer term bonding if you decide that the relationship is worth continuing.

When you meet someone new there are four processes going on:

1) Your internal representation of the meeting – how you feel and think, including thoughts of how you think the other person is thinking about you!

2) Your external representation of the meeting, which is how your body and tone unconsciously communicate what's happening inside. Also represented here are responses to the way they are unconsciously showing you how they feel and think.

3) Their internal representation.

4) Their external representation.

## *Meeting Someone New 101*

**Step 1**                                    **Power Base**

The first thing that someone will notice about you is how confident you are. Your number one key is to find and keep your power base. This gives you confidence anytime and is a strong place to centre yourself to make yourself feel good. Your power base is in your Chi Gung, which is a small area three finger widths below your belly button. Simply bring your attention to that area now (eyes either closed or focused ahead slightly upwards), lift your chin slightly, hold your back straight as though you have elastic attached to the top of your head and breathe. You're instantly becoming calmer and more focused. A brief thought is all that's needed to light it up.

To prove to you just how powerful this area is, do the following exercise with a friend: Have your friend stand with the back of his or her knees or calves against a really cosy armchair or comfortable couch (you're going to push them back onto it, so it needs to be supportive). Stand facing them with your right shoulder to their right shoulder if you are right handed (or vice versa if you are a lefty). Your two shoulders should be about six inches apart. Place your right hand flat on their breastbone in the centre of the chest and say: "I want you to look over my shoulder with your eyes focused up a little and think of your left ear. Let me know as soon as you're there and I'm going to push you back onto the chair. As I do that, resist me as much as you can." It takes a fairly easy push to get them to sit down!

Have the friend stand up again and show them where to find the power centre. Again, ask the person to look over your right shoulder, this time bringing their thoughts to the power base. It's amazingly different. Their resistance is powerful because they are so totally centred. I've easily pushed down a 250lb man when he's thinking left ear and found it not easy to push a 95lb woman when she's thinking of her Chi Gung!

A quicker version of this is to sit opposite a friend and then ask your friend to talk to you while thinking of his/her left ear. Watch the eyes particularly. Then ask them to talk while their attention is in their power base. Notice how much more confident the person looks.

In every situation, whether you're by yourself or meeting someone new, bring your attention to your Chi Gung and your confidence is increased.

**When Meeting Someone New:**

1) Bring your attention to your power base.

2) Walk forward confidently. If you're sitting, simply sit straighter, or stand, as you turn your body to face the other person.

3) Breathe and as you take that breath, raise your eyebrows briefly and open your eyes a little more widely than normal. This eyebrow flash automatically makes the other person feel welcome and acknowledged. You might also give a little half smile, as showing the teeth denotes friendship in Western culture.

4) Turn your body and head in the direction of the other person, (a sign of respect) keeping eye contact as you do so (turning away implies nervousness or inferiority).

5) Lean in slightly towards the person as you show confidence and friendli-

ness with a smile (preferably a wide smile or a series of brief wide smiles if that makes you more comfortable).

Okay, so that's the first ten seconds covered! Yes, I do mean that!

### Step 2          The Greeting

This is where you begin to observe the other person and go along with their model of the world. This is also the formal part of the ritual which moves into words and touch. Part of being human means that you feel more close to someone who touches you, so it's important that you reach out and take the other person's hand as you simply repeat their name (an old politician's trick). This has two effects:

1)  It anchors the person's name and connects it to their face so that you remember who they are and
2)  It makes them feel important (people love to hear the sound of their own name).

The second time you meet someone a brief touch on the upper arm (between the elbow and the shoulder) replaces the handshake and re-establishes familiarity and warmth.

### Step 3          Matching and Mirroring

**Physiology - 55% of communication**
This next bit is the fun part, although it needs to be subtle so that the other person doesn't notice what you're doing and thinks that you're making fun of them.

**Matching - You match the other person's movements exactly.**

> They move their right hand and you move yours a second or so later.
> They cross their legs and so do you.

**Cross-over Matching** – You match a behaviour by crossing over into a similar movement with another part of your body. They cross their legs, you cross your ankles. If someone is blinking rapidly you might cross over match by tapping your finger gently at the same rate.

**Mirroring** – You mirror the other person's movements. They move their left hand to their face, you move your right hand to your face as though you are looking in a mirror.

If you are sitting down with the other person, sit at 90 degrees because that way you are not completely in their vision. Matching and mirroring needs to be just outside their awareness.

You can match:
1) **Posture** – adopt your physiology to theirs. Are they leaning to the right or left? What is the angle of their spine, the tilt of the shoulders or the head? Are their legs crossed? You might cross your ankles. This works well if someone's physiology is not friendly, as in someone's arms being crossed. You could hold your hands with your fingers crossed together to modify their behaviour.

2) **Gestures** – if someone touches their face or hair you can briefly raise your hand to your face a moment or two later. When it's your turn to speak you can copy their gestures. If they have large gestures make yours large. If their gestures are small, tone yours down.

3) **Facial expressions, smiles and eye blinking**. Match their facial expression, including those of sadness, fear or anger. Definitely match smiles briefly and copy blinking patterns, although you need to be careful with this one and only match if the blinking is in the normal range.

4) **Match their breathing pace and location of the breath.** Are they deep or shallow breathers? People breathe out as they talk, so do the same with your breath.

You'll find very quickly that this is an amazingly powerful technique that deepens rapport. You'll also find that you begin to pace and lead the conversation as the other person begins to match and copy your movements.

## Signs of Rapport

1) A feeling inside like butterflies or heartbeat quickening
2) Colour change in the face and neck of both yourself and the other person – a deepening or a flush.
3) Both of you take turns leading and following body language automatically.
4) The other person may say something like: "I feel I've known you a long time." "Haven't we met before?

One of the easiest ways to gain rapport if you're not initially comfortable matching and mirroring, by the way, is to simply tip your head to one side and nod gently while keeping eye contact. This movement shows that you approve of what the person is saying (always nice to know!) and that you're allowing the other person to dominate the conversation. If you wish to speed them up, just nod faster and listen to how quick their language gets. They'll think you're fascinated and will go on and on. It's also natural to briefly look away and back during a conversation so if your eyes begin to water you've probably held the gaze too long!

To get your turn to speak, turn your eyes away and back, your body more upright and perhaps take an obvious breath in as though about to speak. If they still don't catch on you might put up your index finger as though you're in class wanting your turn to answer a question (the baton technique!*). To close the conversation, nod your head as though bowing slightly, mismatch and move your body posture as though you're about to leave and make sure your tone as you speak is in the form of a statement or command (down at the end): "It was great talking to you. Give me a call next week. Bye!"

## Step 4                    Match the other person's voice

### Tonality – 38% of communication

Matching the other person's voice is the quickest way to gain rapport as the voice is the most often outside conscious awareness. When someone is intro- duced to you, the first word will probably be: "Hi" or 'Hello", or "How do you do" in a more formal setting. Match and echo the tone, speed, quality and volume of their greeting exactly and your immediate acceptance is guaranteed. This is easiest to apply on the telephone, when you have no physiology to match. Practice by calling your friend and as the friend answers, match their

*Body Language - Susan Quilliam

tone and words absolutely. The friend will know when it is right because they'll feel more comfortable.

Another way is to sit back to back with someone and repeat something they say with the same depth and resonance like an echo. If you've not exactly got it right they'll feel less comfortable than if you're spot on.

Tone can convey a whole world of meaning. During my post graduate studies at Manchester University in England my classmates were from many different countries as we were studying Teaching English as a Second Language.

We all steered clear of one particular student from Turkey as he always sounded angry. Eventually in one of the discussion groups he asked why no-one liked him. We explained about his 'anger'. He was visibly upset and said that he was not at all angry. We worked out that it was simply his tone of voice. He used a tone which was monotone and staccato, with no modulation. "Put the book on the table please!" can sound very threatening when delivered as a command! He was able to change when I asked him to pretend that he was imitating an English person speaking in an exaggerated manner, with all the inflections and modulations, almost as though he were making fun of us. I knew to do this because my excellent Italian accent was learned by pretending to be an Italian who couldn't speak English very well. The change was miraculous. He became a warm, friendly person overnight!

A friend of mine, Lynn, always acts pleased to see you. Her tone indicates delight as she says your name. It's a special skill to develop which brings pleasure back to you as you remember that person. When I think of Lynn, I hear, "Yvonne!" with a tone going down at the end, rather as though she's saying, "Cookies!" gleefully! It makes me smile as I think of her.

Tone can be conveyed 3 ways:
1) Statement - level voice
2) Question - up at the end
3) Command - down at the end

When you reply to someone, reply with the same inflection on the last 3 or 4 words as they've used with you. Match as closely as possible:

tone (pitch)
tempo (speed) – the most important
timbre (quality)
volume (loudness)

**Step 5**                          **Language**

### Words – 7% of communication

You have the physiology of the person to give you communication clues face to face, but on the phone words need to convey more meaning, so rather than 7%, the importance of the words you use goes up to 18%. This makes the phone a great place to practice, because you'll then become a master wordsmith without the added need to watch body language as you learn to speak and listen to the language of rapport.

As someone picks up the phone, you have even less time to get approval than face-to-face, as you are judged from your very first word! Practice matching that first "Hello" until it becomes automatic to reproduce it exactly. You'll notice that some people talk slowly and some quickly. It's very important that, even if it doesn't sound natural to you, you match their speed and tone.

As a general rule, people can be divided into 4 groups:

1) Visual – tend to talk quickly, voice higher pitched, less distracted by noise, will respond to visual language: "So, do you **see** what I mean?"

2) Auditory – usually have more tonality (a bit like a radio announcer), enjoy talking on the phone, like music, are more easily distracted by noise. They respond to auditory language: "Does that **sound** right to you?"

3) Kinaesthetic – usually 'feel' their world, learn by doing and by trusting their gut feeling. Slower, deliberate phrasing and longer, complicated sentences. "Does that **feel** right to you?"

4) Auditory Digital – the people who self-talk. It has to be logical and make sense to this person to be understood. They think in sequences and like a step-by-step process: "Does that **make sense** to you?"

A good way to remember is that visual/auditory people tend to talk quickly and kinaesthetic/self-talk people talk more slowly. Why is it important to know all this? Because people simply do not compute language that is not in their representational system.

My husband Will (primarily auditory) and I (visual) used to not agree very much until we finally understood why we couldn't communicate well.
We were using our own representational systems to talk to each other.
He would say: "Are you listening to what I'm saying?" and I would reply:
"You're not seeing what I mean". We switched the sentences: He now says:
"Do you see what I mean?" "Yes, I hear you" I reply, and it's as though we actually speak the same language at last.

You might want to listen to the words the other person uses to categorize them into one of the four groups by observing the words they themselves use. Once you've established rapport, you can ease off and the person will still feel comfortable and connected with you.

Here are some examples of how people use the words they relate to in speech:

1) Visual:
   I see. Let me show you another way to look at it to make it more clear.

2) Auditory:
   I hear what you mean. Can I tell you another way that might sound right to you?

3) Kinaesthetic:
   I get your grasp. Let me throw you another idea that might feel better to you.

4) Auditory Digital (self–talk):
   That's an interesting thought. Something's come to my mind that might make more sense to you.

Simply by listening to the words that someone uses, you can find out what their primary representation system is in just a few sentences. Notice one or two key words as they speak and repeat them back in your own sentences. You'll be amazed at how quickly the other person appears to really like you.

There's a whole range of words in each representational system. This list of predicates will help you:

## Representational System Predicates

| VISUAL | AUDITORY | KINAESTHETIC | AUDITORY DIGITAL |
|---|---|---|---|
| See | Hear | Feel | Sense |
| Look | Listen | Touch | Experience |
| Appear | Sound (s) | Grasp | Understand |
| View | Make Music | Get Hold Of | Think |
| Show | Harmonize | Slip Through | Learn |
| Dawn | Tune In/Out | Catch On | Process |
| Reveal | Be All Ears | Tap Into | Decide |
| Envision | Rings A Bell | Make Contact | Motivate |
| Illuminate | Silence | Throw Out | Consider |
| Twinkle | Be Heard | Turn Around | Change |
| Clear | Resonate | Hard | Perceive |
| Foggy | Deaf | Unfeeling | Insensitive |
| Focused | Mellifluous | Concrete | Distinct |
| Hazy | Dissonance | Scrape | Conceive |
| Imagine | Unhearing | Get A Handle | Know |
| Picture | Attune | Solid | Question |
| Sparkling | Outspoken | Suffer | Be Conscious |
| Snap Shot | Tell | Impression | Remember |
| Vivid | Announce | Touch Base | |
| | | Rub | |

© 1995. Tad James, Advanced Neuro Dynamics

## *Language of the Eyes*

You can find out which representational system people use more quickly when you're with someone face-to-face simply by watching their eye movements. Stanford University studied eye pattern movements in the late 70's and discovered that people move their eyes in accordance with whether they're seeing pictures, listening to sounds, accessing their feelings or talking to themselves.

**Visual people** tend to have more eye contact and look up if you ask them to think about something as they look at the picture in their mind (usually up to their left, your right as they're facing you). They usually take care of their appearance as 'looking good' is important. Usually they have good posture and tense shoulders.

**Auditory people** find eye contact not so necessary. They often hold their head to one side without looking at you, as though listening. Their eyes might go horizontally back and forth from ear to ear as they 'listen' inside. They love rhythm and often beat a rhythm on a chair or table. You often see their lips move when thinking, as if they are talking to themselves. The stereo is always on at home or in the car.

**Self-talk people** (auditory digital) look down to your right as you talk to them as they talk to themselves and decide how to respond. They can sometimes appear a bit dissociated and stiff as they live in their heads more than most.

**Kinaesthetic** people look down to your left as you look at them as they access how they feel about things. They tend to be rounder, more relaxed individuals with fuller lips and body posture that leans in a round shouldered way. They breathe more deeply; have a relaxed manner and a deep voice. Clothes are chosen for comfort rather than fashion.

When you use the person's own model or way of experiencing the world, communication is smoother and rapport is established very quickly. The other person feels that you know them at a very deep level and will remember you.

One thing to note about children: Children who are not finding it easy to learn may just have a different representational system than their teacher's. Kinaesthetic children particularly may be accessing how they felt when a word was introduced to them! Auditory children may be trying to access the sound of the word instead of the picture. Write down the word 'SUCCESS' (written half in red and half in blue) and hold it up and to the left of the child's face, just above eye level to teach the child how to access the information correctly (visual recall area). Ask the child to spell it out, then close their eyes and spell it. You can have fun by asking the child to spell the word backward too! Teach the child to do this trick whenever they need to learn a new word, or teach them to hold the book just above eye level when learning new information.

# THE SIXTH KEY-

## The Power of RELATIONSHIPS

Once you have established the ability to communicate with yourself and others, it's time to improve your relationships so that you feel more connected. It's what we all want and need on some level – love, happiness, romance and unconditional acceptance. It's a need to belong, feel safe and just be able to be ourselves which is a need common to animals and humans, males and females, rich and poor. Part of being human is the need to feel integrated and aligned with universal and corporal love. Why is it then that we sometimes feel isolated or not attached?

Because to some extent, all of us have areas of our character like this:

**A pie with a piece missing:**

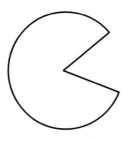

So …like attracts like, remember? All you can attract in when your pie is not complete is another pie with a bit missing:

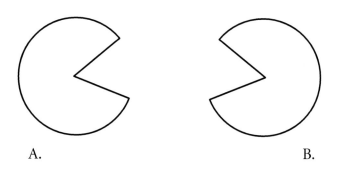

A.　　　　　　　　　　　　　　　　B.

### Hands up, all you caretakers, caregivers or enablers! (A)

A. says: "I recognize you! You're just like me!" (or, more simply put, "I really fancy you!") "Let me help you fill that hole with love, care, cooking. I'll organize your bank balance, help you get a job, change hats to be whatever you want me to be."

B. (the receiver) says: "Thanks very much!" The thing that's not fortunate is that B's hole is only going to be filled temporarily, and to fill B's pie, you have to use some more of your own pie. Thus:

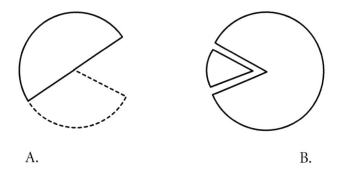

A.　　　　　　　　　　　　　　　　B.

This is how co-dependency happens. You feel better when you're with B, because B. has your stuff (i.e. all the time and effort you've spent trying to make the relationship work). You do not feel good when you're away from B., because B. has all your stuff.

In the Celestine Prophecy, the explanation about relationships is that each person is half a circle looking for the other half. Aristophanes, the Greek comic and poet, also said that each person is half of a single unit of love; that the goal is to find the other half. I don't believe that's true. When we each complete our own circle, we can then attract in someone else who is also a complete circle. Thus:

Attraction

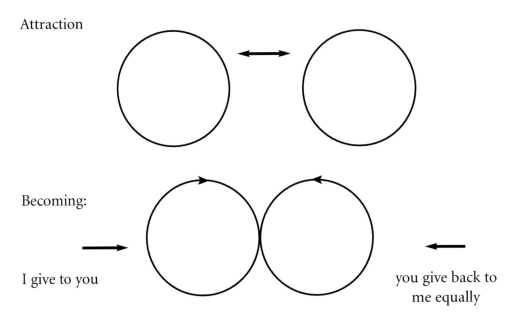

Becoming:

I give to you                                                    you give back to
                                                                      me equally

The figure above is also the symbol for infinity, and the number 8, which in numerology is the number of power, money, success and self-worth.

When I was 39 years old, I decided to change my life. I had been a clairvoyant, palmist and card reader for many years, had been a teacher in Italy and South Africa, sold real estate, studied aromatherapy massage, been married and divorced, travelled all over the world and been on T.V. and radio, but had never really felt as though I had a home anywhere, even though I owned a house in England.

I realized that what was missing was a decent relationship and children. I had been doing breath therapy (rebirthing) for three years to clear old issues and finally decided that I was ready to settle down. My timeline was short, as my biological clock was ticking, so I sat down one day and thought a lot about how I chose relationships.

My pattern was this: Because I love to heal, the guy had to need major help, or I lost interest very quickly! He usually had to be not doing well financially because then I could help him out. It really helped if he was looking for solutions around drink or drugs. I decided to change my attitude. I would go out to the usual dances, clubs and pick out the men I was attracted to and then say to myself, "Okay, I like you, you and you. You men must be needy! Let's talk to someone else!" I would then choose the most decent-looking man in the room i.e. self-confident, didn't have "Help!" written all over his forehead, and would go and talk to him. It took me a while to get used to the idea, but eventually I came to like the fact that I was learning for a change, not teaching.

I began to be very selective with the dates. Just to get a first date the man had to have a decent job, own his own house and work with people, not things (if I was to be pregnant I didn't want to have to work up to the date of the birth!). I also wanted to have someone who valued himself, had made a commitment to life and self-growth and had a sense of humour!

As time went by, I speeded up the process by going out with someone for just three dates. I would tell him that he had three dates to prove himself. On the fourth date he would ask, "Does this mean that I have to marry you?" I would reply, "No, you just got a fourth date. Don't push your luck!" I had half a dozen rings offered to me that year because I was so cheeky. It was also great fun.

When I actually met my future husband, Will, he walked into the apartment, looked at me and said, "You're marrying me and having my child. Did you know that?" Yes, I did know. There was a reaction that was like a lightning bolt when we hugged for the first time. You need to feel that 'click'.
 If you've ever watched dating programs on TV you can see within seconds of the couple meeting for a 'blind date' whether they will be seeing each other again. No matter how 'suitable' they appear to be for each other, that 'click' has to occur. Chemistry's a wonderful thing.

### Is there just one Mr. or Miss. Right for me?

You may have many possible partners this lifetime. At different points of your life, you will come to a 'hot pink' point when relationships just seem to happen. Just as described in numerology and astrology, at various time periods in your life, different aspects; career, money, health, home, romance or family will be emphasized.

You will get less and less happy emotionally as these time points approach in order to stimulate you to change. You will then be given choices. You may, for instance, find that a wonderful job offer to travel and make a home elsewhere comes in just as you meet who you think may be Mr. (or Mrs.) Right.  Make the incorrect choice and you may delay your life for a number of years.  Make the correct choice (the one which 'resonates' or feels right, even if it is not easy) and life will offer amazing gifts; periods of your life when everything seems to go right. Timing is very important to align synchronicity.

## *Time and Timing*

A number of years ago, there was a wonderful Timex watch advertisement on the TV: Miss Smith was walking along the street loaded up with parcels.  Mr. Jones was at right angles to her, just about to cross the street.  The advert then showed the future: he was going to bump into her, take her for a coffee by way of an apology, then marry her, live in a lovely house, have kids, and live happily ever after. Then it reverted back to the present and the anticipation of the meeting. The advert went a bit like "Jaws" as Mr. Jones approached Miss Smith: "Dah duh, dah duh, dah duh, dah duh!"............ and just as he reached her, he went right behind her and into a shop doorway. The end of the advert stated, "He should've been wearing a Timex watch!"

That advert describes exactly how relationships work.  We need to trust the 'just missed' effect and move on from a relationship when it's not working instead of giving it six weeks, six months, six years, or six lifetimes! Unfortunately, all of us have at some point hung around in the shop doorway waiting for an unsuitable person instead of moving on to the next 'click point'. Kiss as many frogs (or frogesses) as you can as quickly as you can so that you can find the right one sooner!

# The Marriage Connection

## SOULMATES AND TWIN FLAMES

Why is it that we have a deep need to marry or make a promise to stay with someone? Because:

*"Marriage is our last, best chance to grow up"*

JOHN BAITLE

You marry your unconscious mind.
Let me repeat that – You marry your unconscious mind.
That means that any area of your life which is not in harmony will surface the further you go into a marriage, in order to be worked on and then cleared.

I use the word marriage to mean a commitment or a union between two people, including common-law situations and gay relationships. It's an honouring of the other person and a sharing of mutual goals which will benefit both. Marriage, to me, is a sacred promise. Will, my husband will say to me when we start talking about petty things: "We promised on our wedding day that we wouldn't do this." It brings me up short and takes me immediately back to that lovely day when I felt like a Princess.

Is your intent to have your partner understand you and help you or is it your intent that you should both help each other? In a win/win situation both partners need to be involved. I love watching Will change and become more confident, more self-aware and happier every year. I remember one evening when Will and I were standing at the front door shouting at each other over something trivial (it usually is, isn't it?). "Okay!" he said "Do you want me to leave right now and get an apartment? Is that what you want? Because I will!" "No" I replied "I just want you to be a part of making this marriage work!" "Okay" he said "Do you want a cup of tea?" He walked into the kitchen and whatever was not right was gone! Both of us needed to hear the other's intention of staying together.

So how do you keep the marriage alive and growing through the years?
One important way is to make sure that you both have outside interests and a sense of purpose in life both individually and collectively. Keeping a sense of

humour is essential too!

## Date Night

It's sometimes not easy to communicate well, especially when both of you are working and there are children, animals, and other friends around.  That's why, just when you think there's no time left in the week, you need a date night. A time when you can spend time alone with each other.

When Will and I are aware that we are feeling less close, we take off for just one night to a local hotel.  We play scrabble, go to the cinema, go out to eat and talk.  It's wonderful to do ordinary things together again. The intimacy of spending real time together also renews the passion.

## Praise and Validate

In that first flush of love, we praise, praise, praise!
"I like you because you're so handsome and talented.  You're great with people, you know.  I love being with you." can turn to: "It's your turn to take out the garbage. Oh, and you could move those socks and shoes you left in the hall on your way out. Thanks."

Do this:
When you're together, or on your date night one evening, ask, "What do you like about me still?" (If the partner says "I like….. but" tell him/her to edit the buts – pure praise please!) It makes your partner remember why he/she chose to be with you in the first place, instead of thinking about what you're not doing.

If you feel sometimes that you are not communicating fully, say something nice to your other half instead of anything that was about to come out!
This is not easy sometimes, I know! It opens a door where all exits were closed.

Will and I have three main keys that we apply:

1) Both of us have 24 hours to talk about something which is not making us happy, then after that it's not valid and not listened to! This rule makes sure that we can't hold a grudge (and it really works).

2) We always use high-energy words when we talk to each other.
   We state how we feel, not what we think the other person should do.

3) We create random acts of kindness to make the other person feel special every day.

In order for a relationship to continue to work, two things need to happen: Your feelings about the other person need to stay positive, and the love strategies of both partners need to remain fulfilled. That means that you should both know what to do or say to make the other person feel loved. How do you find that out? You simply ask what's important to them about love and intimacy. Get specific with this one. It's the small things that make a difference.

Finally……
If the relationship really isn't working; if one of you has grown away or the resentment is too deep, give it a 'sell by' or 'best before' date, but tell the partner first. "I'm really not happy with our relationship. Do you want it to continue like this, or are you willing to work with me to see if we can improve it by this summer/ Christmas / Hanukkah?" Putting in an actual time frame implies that the relationship will be reviewed or finished by that date, so that both of you can move on.

The best marriages that I have seen are those where each partner delights in the other's accomplishments and achievements. The phrase usually begins: "I am so proud of him/her because…" We are always proud of and boasting about our children. It would be lovely to validate our marriage relationships the same way.

## Children – Our Key to the Future

*"Your children are not your children. They are the sons and daughters of Life's longing for itself. They come through you but not from you.*
*And though they are with you they belong not to you.*
*You are the bows from which your children as living arrows are sent forth."*
KAHLIL GIBRAN – THE PROPHET

Our children hold the key to the future of humanity and it's by teaching them about how to communicate well in relationships that you can ensure their happiness.

Celine Dion, who appeared to have it all: looks, money, success, romance and fame, after having a child said: "It's like life holds a secret and having a child is that secret."

It's a privilege to be a parent, one I truly appreciate because I had to wait so long to have a child. I was forty-two when I had Katherine Louise and Will was forty-eight (we were 90 between us!). I talked to Katie from the moment she was conceived (actually, it was probably before that!) I would walk in the sunshine and tell her about the breeze I could feel against my face. I would get in the bath and splash water noisily and tell her how much she would love the water (she adores it.) I did some breath work therapy to prepare for the birth and release my own fear.

When she was four-years-old, I asked her casually if she remembered being born. "Yes – it was dark and then it was light." "Do you remember the nice music that was playing?" I asked. "No – but I remember it smelled lovely. My bum was really sore for three days. And I remember daddy talking." Will had held her for two hours after her birth, telling her about how he was going to take her on swings in the park and play with her. We had aromatherapy oils to massage me during the labour and the nurses kept coming in just to smell the room. Katie had been born bottom first (a frank breech) and her little bottom was black and blue with all the pulling to get her out. It also surprised me that she knew somehow that it had been three days exactly when the bruising started to fade.

Children remember a great deal between three and four years old. The 'new' personality then begins to integrate and the memories fade. Katie has no recollection of her birth now. At some point in her life before she has her own children, I would like to take her back to remember her birth and clear any low-energy emotions around the experience, so that she can erase the genetic memory (apparently Will was also born frank breech with a dislocated left shoulder, just as Katie was).

I would always talk to Katie as though she understood everything I said. Even when she was a tiny baby, when I left a room I would always tell her I was leaving and would be back (she never had the abandonment issues other children seemed to have). Before she could walk she managed to find her way up three flights of stairs to the top of the house. We worked for the next two weeks teaching her how to come down safely rather than put gates everywhere.

I edited almost everything I was about to say to Katie after she was born. I did not use the word, "No" and truly questioned "Why not?" When Katie wanted to pee like a dog in the yard, she peed! When she wanted to wear no coat for the first snow, I held the coat ready for her cries of "Where's my coat?" She's self-confident and passionate about life, she's popular, she's creative, and she loves people and exploring new boundaries. She's funny, laughs a lot and is more sensitive as she learns to control her emotions. We've always told her that she can do anything she sets her mind on doing. It's a pleasure and a privilege for us to know her.

## *We are the Keepers of the Sacred Space*

It's a fact that every child believes that their dreams will come true. Your children (or any children you meet) are your opportunity to show that you are ready to trust, that you believe, that you yourself find life wonderful. Every moment that you spend with that child could be the moment that the child recognizes his or her own beauty and power. Can you search inside and ask the one question that could lead the child to a realization that they are an exquisite learner, or that their ideas are great or that they made a very informed choice that turned out well? Can you accept a child's behaviour as an expression of the child's individuality? Can you simply ask "Why?" when a child acts out and see humour in the situation? Focus on the act, not the child, look for the solution, not the punishment, because punishing simply 'anchors' the low-energy behaviour even more strongly than before. Ask the child what he or she could do differently to get a happier result. Children know. They are in touch with deep inner wisdom.

**Not Acceptable**

a) Behaviour that is not safe to him/herself.
b) Behaviour that is not safe to someone else.
c) Behaviour that intrudes on someone else's space.

**Acceptable**

**Everything else.**

# *Discover Yourself Through Your Child*

You have a chance to change your own future through your children, as they show you a mirror image of your unresolved issues. Remember that your unconscious mind is listening and making notes. It believes that everything you tell the child is something that you believe about yourself. Make it different and make a difference.

As well as taking every chance to praise, praise and praise some more, be playful and funny when you need to let the child know that changes in behaviour are needed. Think outside the box. Your total attention is needed to establish rapport and trust (turn the cell phone off when you are spending time with the child!). Let the child know that you really like him or her.

We are born into this world with endless possibilities. We are radiant beings longing for unconditional love and acceptance. We begin our lives in perfect freedom and with loving, supportive parents we become the best we can be. When you were born you began a journey that was an exciting journey into the unknown. It was about searching for love, fulfillment and belonging. It was about comfort and feeling safe. It was about learning, growing and just being. You reinvented yourself every day before you were seven years old, during the 'imprinting' phase. Every day was a new day, every person you met and every event had a profound effect on how you saw yourself. Somewhere along the line you began to become an observer, noticing the classical physical (Newtonian) laws as they were pointed out to you by other people or as you discovered them e.g. Action has an equal and opposite reaction. Smile and someone smiles back at you. If you knock a glass from the table, it may break. A three-year-old simply thinks that it makes an interesting noise as it breaks. The caring adult will make sure that the child does not have access to a glass again until such time as the child can understand the reason for being careful. A less enlightened adult may yell, scare the child and sometimes even punish, at which point the child will learn something and come to a decision. Perhaps that it's not safe to touch glass. Perhaps that it's not safe to touch things on the table. Perhaps it's that adults are scary for no good reason! Perhaps even that it's not safe to try anything new. Or all of those things! Eventually, enough low-energy experiences and instructions can impact the way a child (and later the adult) thinks about and responds to life. The low-energy voice inside is the inner dialogue which sabotages success because it blocks the communication channel from the source of abundance. The less happy someone is, the more fragmented and unstable they become, taking them further away from what they want to have, or be, or do.

# How to Really Love a Child

*Be there. Say yes as often as possible. Let them bang on pots and pans. If they're crabby, put them in water. If they're unlovable, love yourself. Realize how important it is to be a child. Go to a movie theatre in your pyjamas. Read a book out loud with joy. Invent pleasures together. Remember how really small they are. Giggle a lot. Surprise them. Say no only when necessary. Teach feelings. Heal your own inner child. Learn about parenting. Hug trees together. Make loving safe. Bake a cake and eat it with no hands. Go find elephants and kiss them. Plan to build a rocket ship. Imagine yourself magic. Make lots of forts with blankets. Let your angel fly. Reveal your own dreams. Search out the high-energy. Keep the gleam in your eye. Mail letters to God. Encourage silliness. Plant liquorice in your garden. Open up. Stop yelling. Express your love. A lot. Speak kindly. Paint their tennis shoes. Handle with care. Children are miraculous.*

WRITTEN BY THE AUTHOR SARK.

With years of intuitive readings behind me, I've learned that we seem to 'choose' our children and they 'choose' us*. It's as though an agreement or contract is made before we enter life that we will help so many children. For instance, a woman can have two children, a boy and a girl, written in her hand as destiny, and then have none. But she will have a niece and nephew who are very close. Similarly, if someone has three children in their hand and then only has two, the third may be a grandchild who will be adored.

I'll always remember during one breath therapy session a man who called out: "I wasn't meant to be your son! I should have been your brother! It was grandma's job to have me, not yours! No wonder you're such a lousy mother!" By releasing his low-energy emotions he was able to come to terms with the fact that he felt he'd 'missed out'. His relationships with both women improved after this, by the way.

About six months before conception occurs, the future child appears to go into a waiting or 'holding' area. As conception becomes imminent, the child

*'The Eternal Journey' - (a chronicle of near-death experiences)
Craig R. Lundahl / Harold A.Widdison, gives examples of children who didn't get parents of their choice.

appears, seeming to be around two years old in size and standing to the left of the woman. It's as though the child has to return to a lower vibration before it can enter the new body. They quite clearly show themselves to be male or female. In my therapy sessions I have taken hundreds of people back to before birth, back to the moment of conception. Asked what lesson they are to learn, the client's answers are simple:

"To love and be loved."
"To be self-reliant."
"To care for others."
"To learn to receive."
"To overcome difficulty."
"To learn that life's not always easy."

To achieve their full potential, children need to be loved and accepted completely by parents who love themselves and each other. Happiness and self-worth is all about love.

*Love*

| **UNCONDITIONAL** | **CONDITIONAL** |
|---|---|
| praise, encouragement guidance, acceptance | criticism, restriction, control, judgement |
| ... empowerment leads to expression | ... disempowerment leads to repression |
| **which results in** passion, power, humour focus, security, trust (feeling in control) | **which results in** anger, guilt, fear, sadness, shame, doubt, distrust, (feeling overwhelmed) |
| pro-active mentality | victim mentality |
| **...leads to** making active choices (high-energy) | **...leads to** making reactive choices (low-energy) |
| action, participation, integration | inaction, withdrawal, isolation, separation |
| **...resulting in** creativity, construction success, enthusiasm self-confidence | **...resulting in** apathy, destruction, depression self-destruction (obsession, compulsion, addiction) |

(Way Out)

| AWARE | NOT AWARE |
|---|---|
| EXPANSION INTO POWER | CONTRACTION INTO PAIN |
| **GOOD HEALTH** | **NOT GOOD HEALTH** |

In regression therapy, people go back to pre-birth and pre-conception to enable them to see their parents as individuals outside and separate from themselves. In every single case (no exceptions so far) the person has clear pre-birth and pre-conception memories!

I ask clients to go back to three months before their conception to find their birth mother: "She's so young!" "She's so beautiful!" "She doesn't look happy!" "She's worn out!" "She's expecting me!" "There are problems in the relationship already." When they find their birth father: "He's happy." "He's handsome." "He's feeling responsible." "He's depressed about money."

Asked if they like their birth mother/father, the responses vary from:
"I love her/him", "I don't like her/him" to "I'm coming to help her/him".
The separation of the client's own feelings from parents' feelings leads to more healthy adult relationships.

*'Our birth is but a sleeping and a forgetting.'*
WORDSWORTH

**Why do we not remember this experience until we are regressed?**

According to the Kabbalah, an angel is supposed to stand by the soul as it is about to enter the mother's body. A discussion takes place about what is to happen, and then the angel places a finger of forgetfulness on the upper lip of the child, so that the child will come into the life with hope and freedom of choice. Although I was told the identity of my child before she was born and was excited about telling her, I was given strict instructions that she was not to know. Her slate was to be clean to allow her to have free will.

It would appear that we commit to a definite number of children (or souls that we have promised to help grow) with a number of extra possibilities. For instance, Katie is someone I knew, whom I had already made a commitment to help. The second child was a 'choice' child. He would have loved the chance to come in, but didn't make it. By the time we tried to have another child, my fertility was very low. At 46 years old, the chances were not good. Katie amazed me about six months ago. "Mom," she said, "Who was the boy who was trying to get into your body?" "I think he was meant to be your brother, darling."

"That's okay" Katie replied, "He can be my son instead!"

One of my own most powerful therapy sessions was when I entered the pre-conception state spontaneously. I was standing with a lady dressed in white, who was holding my left hand (age-wise, I was around two or three years old). I remember being very surprised at how much my father adored my mother and how good-looking they were as a couple. I was reluctant to enter because I knew that it was not an easy task that I was about to undertake. The less easy the childhood seems to be, the greater the possibility for achievement and making a difference as an adult. The lady looked down at me and said, "It's your choice, you know. You really don't have to do this." I still hesitated. Three or four guides standing behind me said, "We'd really appreciate it if you go in. We'll also be with you to help, even though you won't be aware of us." The lady then scooped me up in a kind of energy vortex and slid me into my mother's body, saying "Happy Birthday" as she did so.

The most wonderful feeling came from this recollection: I had actually 'chosen' to come here in order to help others. I no longer felt a 'victim of fate' and was aware of a sense of oneness and belonging that I had never known before. I still have that feeling.

I've since taken clients back to this moment. Guides have been male or female. The guides always seem to make a little comment as the baby is conceived, like: "Good luck!" or "You're safe."

## *Love Life – Live Longer*

*"There is no true solitude except interior solitude."*

THOMAS MERTON.

As parents our job is to guide and help to teach a child to manage the strong emotions and feelings that accompany childhood. Disapproval results in feelings of isolation and eventual repression of feelings as the child tries to constantly win the parent's affection by 'behaving'.

## *Fear is Misdirected Power. Anger is Misdirected Passion.*

All the "No's!" and "Don'ts!" directed in childhood can result in feelings of anger or frustration as the child learns to use the limbic or emotional brain. When she was younger, Katie used to shout at me: "I hate you! You're the worst parent in the world!", and I'd reply: "That's okay, I still love you, and you're still not having candies before you go to bed!" It didn't bother me when she showed strong emotion because I knew that she was simply showing strong emotion. It was also fun to reply, "Thanks Katie! A silver medal for me today!" I got a gold medal when I was the worst parent in the Universe!

However, if she hit out, that was another thing altogether because:

1)  It was intruding into my (or someone else's) space and
2)  It was not a good way to express frustration.

I found other ways for her to direct the energy. A five minute time out, beating a pillow, a run around the garden, followed by a dose of calmag (Floradix make a pleasant tasting liquid Calmag) to relax her and help process the anger. Directing the anger into creativity (painting, drawing, etc.) also gives a child a way to direct strong feelings when the child grows up. There's a fine line between over-controlling and not guiding at all which is not easy to draw. However, over-controlling parents produce children with control issues. Children absorb not only our strengths, our capacities and our talents, but also our less strong qualities, our confusions and limitations.

We support Katie's self-concept and down play when she guilt-trips herself, asking her what lesson could she draw from the event instead. We make fair rules - cleaning up her own room, tidying after she has played. I don't give her 'chores' to do – she'll have plenty of time for them when she has her own household.  I do sometimes say: "Do you want to help me make the eggs / show you how to work the washer / use the vacuum cleaner?" She still loves to help, because it never became 'work'. Her allowance is unconditional – not based on jobs.  It was her idea to have one dollar for every year of her life.  At present she gets ten dollars every Saturday.  She saves some money every week for buying other people gifts, so that she can understand budgeting.

Our children need to have better opportunities than us – we already have money aside for Katie's college fund so that she won't have to work at something else while at university. Children need our love and acceptance, our attention, support, the freedom of choice and the teaching of a gradual responsibility. A child will be and achieve exactly what you expect him or her to be – he/she will thrive with praise and support and acceptance and wither with criticism, judgement or disappointment – just like us adults, funnily enough.

## *Safe Place Exercise*

Night time is sometimes not easy for a child, especially as children have such fertile imaginations. They are more connected to the unconscious mind so the mind releases daily emotional build up more quickly and easily. Establish this five minute exercise as a routine so that you get a good night's sleep!

Hold the child's hand and say softly: "Close your eyes. Let's pretend.
Okay, we're going to find a safe place in nature for you to go. Would you like a seaside and beach, or a mountain or a lovely forest of trees, or a tree house in the garden? Tell me about the place. Imagine the birds singing, the sun shining warmly on your skin. Can you hear any water? See how clear the colours are. Is there someone to play with? Who else is there? Are there any animals? What's happening now?" Make as few suggestions as you can to detail the scene because the child needs to use his/her own creativity and imagination as much as possible. Children will normally go to the same place again and again and replay the same scene over and over with just small variations.

Angels of protection are a lovely image to present to a child. We all seem to relate to angels and angels are cross-cultural. Paint them on the walls of the child's room or ceiling and name them. Katie has a dog angel that she drew on the ceiling over her head! Decorative dream catchers are another way to make the child feel safe.

### *Less than Happy dreams*

Once the safe place five minutes is established as a ritual, you can get the child to go there immediately if a disturbing dream occurs. I normally ask Katie to describe the least happy part of the dream e.g. a monster, then ask her how does she think we can try and clear it out? Should we get super dog to come and take it away?  Shrink it into a small box? The last time this happened she put the now small monster into a box, set it onto the water in a boat and pushed the boat off to sea. This teaches a child to find an immediate solution to a scary or uneasy situation, which will give the child great coping tools for later on in life.

# The Language of Parenthood
## -12 Keys

**1)        Find other ways of saying "No!"**

"If you play with daddy's glasses, they may break – here play with this lovely ball." It's not as easy as saying "No!', however the child will actually listen when you say 'no' later in childhood.

**Not Acceptable:**

a)  Behaviour that is not safe to him/herself.
b)  Behaviour that is not safe to someone else.
c)  Behaviour that intrudes on someone else's space.

**Acceptable**

*Everything else.*

**2)        Always keep a promise.**

I've had many clients who have spent years getting over childhood disappointments.

**3)        Always tell the truth (no hidden agendas).**

"Yes, daddy and I are not agreeing and that's okay – it's better to talk things through."  Children pick up on non-verbal messages much more then we realize. They pick up quickly if a relationship isn't working.

## 4)        Explain, explain, and explain!

Fear of the unknown is the least easy part of childhood. When we talk down to a child or dismiss their fears, things can quickly get disproportionate. Katie and I talk about her dreams every morning. "What does it mean mom?" is usually followed by, "Well, who do you think is the scary cat? Did you let someone upset you yesterday?" Katie's getting quite adept at realizing what each person or animal represents and is able to talk through her fears, understanding the lessons and letting the emotions go.

## 5)        Always apologize. Forgiveness is the language of self-love.

The ability to apologize to the child shows inner strength and an ability to be accountable. Both are great qualities to teach a child.

## 6)      Tackle things head on! Talk it through.

Major issues for a child can be divorce of parents, a death in the family, illness or financial problems. Just as major is a house move, mom or dad starting a new job, a new baby, even a new teacher or a new school year. When my sister died when I was 13, I remember hearing people say, "Yes, Yvonne is taking it really well – she's back to normal now" – this was only a couple of months after her death! I remember thinking that I was screaming inside and that no one could hear. When people asked "How are you dear?" I would always say "I'm fine!" So fine, in fact, that I cried myself to sleep for years and slept with the light on, afraid to go to sleep (in case I died too) for more then twelve months after her death.

## 7)        No sarcasm or making fun of a child – they take everything literally. Treat the child with respect and dignity.

At eleven years old I was told by my father that because I passed my 11 plus exam with flying colours they must have marked the wrong exam paper! It took me six years to realize that I had made it to grammar school through my own efforts.

## 8)        Can we make something fun? Play is great for both of you.

There are opportunities to make everything fun – it takes more energy, and it's worth it. I love having parties for both children and adults. When someone says "You've worked so much" I reply: "No, working is doing an evening meal day after day, year after year – this is great!"

## 9)     Allow the child choice.

I remember one day when I was trying to help Katie become more independent. "You can choose what you'd like to wear today," I said.
"This mommy!" She picked out a really pretty summer dress.
"No darling, it's winter – that won't be good to wear today."
"Okay – this" she picked out another outfit.
"Those colours really don't go together, sweetie."
Katie started to get upset. I suddenly heard a voice from the bedroom saying "What about choose but you have no choice really?" (Will had been listening). I was not happy with myself. She wore the colourful outfit that day and after that I would take two or three suitable outfits, lay them out and she would choose one of them, thus giving her a sense of independence with my approval.

## 10)    No loud voices or shouting. No physical punishment.

All the studies are unanimous. Corporal punishment is a huge risk factor for poor school results, alienation from the family group and adult violence. A study from the American Medical Association News Update a few years ago suggests that one cause of bullying is spanking. They followed 800 mothers from varying social groups and found that children who were spanked, even once a week in an otherwise loving and emotionally warm family, all showed an increase in anti-social behaviour, a tendency to cheat and lie, bullying, cruelty to others and disobedience at school*.
Controlling emotional and physical punishment teaches a child nothing about boundary setting and everything about submission or rebellion in the presence of an authority figure. Ultimately that repressed anger has to go somewhere! If it's not expressed outwardly, the child or future adult will hurt or abuse themselves instead.

*Michelle Landsberg – article on violence – The Toronto Star, March 31. 2002.
Dr. Susan Turner's book Something to Cry About, an Argument against Corporal Punishment of Children in Canada has many case studies directly correlating physical punishment of children to their levels of aggression in adulthood.

### 11)      Validate.

Children, like pregnant women, often don't need 'fixing'. They just need to be told that it's okay (and healthy) to express and release emotions.
 "Even though" is a good phrase to remember – "Even though you're not feeling happy the doctors are here to make you well."

### 12)      Praise, praise and praise some more. And hug, hug and hug again.

Eliminate the word "but" when you praise a child (or anyone for that matter!). "That's lovely, but you haven't done the tree right!" Do you think the child really heard the "that's lovely" part? Criticism is never constructive, always destructive. You can correct without criticizing: "Wow! That drawing is awesome! Do you want me to show you how it could be even better? Here, I'll draw it on this paper and you can copy it if you'd like." If the child doesn't copy it, that's fine – they'll observe and remember next time.

One important thing to note is that parents often use the child's name when they disapprove of something. They'll often use 'honey' or 'sweetie' or 'angel' instead of the child's name when approving! I asked my child's classmates how many of them like their name and only three of them did!

If your child is not easy to handle, has a short attention span, does not like sleeping or staying asleep, you might look at food allergies as a possible cause (see section on physical health). It's been proven that 75% of North Americans have a magnesium deficiency, so consider adding Calmag (calcium/magnesium combo) to your child's diet. Floradix do a fruity liquid calmag and I recently found a fruity fizzy Calmag that Katie prefers. I find that when she takes this regularly, she doesn't get as emotional, and she sleeps though the night much more solidly. Her immune system has been dramatically improved since she started the multivitamins (for kids) and the Calmag.

Children are far wiser than adults in many ways. I asked Kate yesterday what she thought was the recipe for happiness. She replied:
"Be true to yourself. Be kind to others. Have fun."

# THE SEVENTH KEY
## The Power of SPIRITUAL CONNECTION

Spiritual health is vital to your well-being because there needs to be an awareness of something greater than yourself in order for you to be at peace in your heart. Spiritual health is about learning to trust, even when you feel you have reasons not to trust. It's about opening yourself up to the idea that sometimes simple acceptance is stronger than any amount of questioning.

This was brought home to me when I was in my twenties. I was alone in a dark room, having just been told that my then husband had just been seen with another woman. There I was in South Africa, six thousand miles away from home, feeling as though I was the only person in the world who had ever felt like I was feeling then. I was too shocked to cry and it was almost as though my breath was still. There was no noise except my heart beating. I asked, "Why?" over and over again. Quite slowly the room began to glow. Light began to pour in from all around, and I watched with amazement as a lady in white emerged. She just looked at me with compassion, and then faded away. Her presence gave me a sense of safety. I felt my heart release and open up and I slept peacefully, knowing that it was time to accept that the relationship was over.

What is important is that healing of the spiritual body is a 'do with', not a 'do to', process. Whatever or whoever you believe in; spiritual harmony is achieved by recognizing that there is something more to life than what your five senses tell you. It's the development of the sixth sense, the higher consciousness that takes you to a new level of understanding. Physical sciences deal with our physical reality, so why is it that all great physicists embrace some sort of mysticism?

Perhaps because, as Sir James Jeans pointed out:
*"Physicists who are trying to understand nature may work in many different fields and by many different methods; one may dig, one may sow, one may reap. But the final harvest will always be a sheaf of mathematical formulae. These will never describe nature itself......"*

# The Big Picture

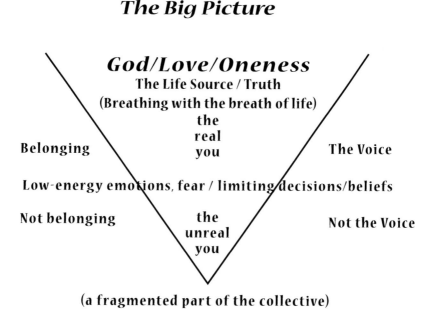

**God/Love/Oneness**
The Life Source / Truth
(Breathing with the breath of life)
the real you

Belonging        The Voice

Low-energy emotions, fear / limiting decisions/beliefs

Not belonging        the unreal you        Not the Voice

(a fragmented part of the collective)

You can choose to have your point of consciousness above or below the line.

Albert Einstein said that a man's experience is an optical delusion of his consciousness, meaning that what we perceive to be 'reality' is totally subjective. You might think of this as though you are looking at yourself in a mirror (the real you). The 'you' that is looking back at you from the glass is not real, although it looks as though there is someone else there. Have you ever watched a small child catch sight of himself and then go around the back of the mirror to look for the other child? Sometimes as adults we don't remember that fear, low-energy emotions and limiting beliefs are illusion too.

Anything other than God is not God and as God is Love, then anything other than God or Love is not 'real'. Why is this important to understand? Because:

### *You can only receive presents from God when you're in the presence of God.*

We know that negativity creates separation and polarity as it creates dissociation from the oneness.

*"Dissociation is nothing more than a decision to forget! What has been forgotten then appears to be fearful, but only because the dissociation is an attack on truth"*

COURSE IN MIRACLES

Removal of the low-energy voice, which is represented by low-energy emotions such as anger, sadness, fear and guilt, and limiting decisions and beliefs, allows you to access and dialogue with the inner or real you. This releases the boundaries to bring you to the realization that there is no separation. Using life-affirming words connects you with the high-energy voice and the true voice inside, thus making a quantum leap forward to access abundance and joy on every level.

You are light, goodness and truth. You are already home. This 'coming home' is what we all are searching for. The connection with universal truth brings you to the inner treasure, the Holy Grail. The freedom to be yourself.

*"Believe as a child believes, and the magic will find you".*

THERESA LANGDON

Then you can be, do, or have whatever you want just by sending out a thought.

There have always been great teachers willing to show the way to God, should anyone choose to listen. Buddha, Jesus, Mohammed and Abraham were just some of the spiritual masters; part of the universal brotherhood of teachers who help and heal humanity.

At various stages of your development, you will become aware of 'guides' or 'spirits' helping you to reach the higher spheres. You will only progress at your own rate, although by meditation and helping others your progression can be speeded up. With the correct directed effort you can tap the bounteous energy of the universal power. Your life is a painting; you are the artist. By opening the flow of psychic energy in your life, you can transform what would have been a very ordinary picture into a masterpiece.

Carl Gustav Jung's study of primitive tribes led him to believe that there is a vast hidden store of images common to all of mankind, regardless of race or creed. He called this the 'collective unconscious'; a storehouse of knowledge which can be 'tapped' by tuning in to a frequency higher than normal.

Let's take a look at how we connect and interact with one another from a spiritual perspective:

### 1. Two Strangers

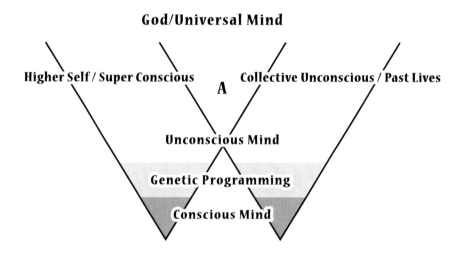

In Figure 1, the space that two strangers share (who will never meet) can be likened to space A. Their actions will be recorded on a higher level, or higher vibration, than their awareness, in the space we call the 'collective unconscious' or 'super conscious' (also known as the Akashic Records) and of course on a higher level still – God or the Universal Mind.

Rupert Sheldrake discovered that self-organizing living things (from molecules to entire galaxies) are shaped by Morphic Fields; they have morphic resonance i.e. every time we learn something it is passed on to the rest of humanity immediately, rather like a cumulative and collective memory. This explains how two scientists can and often do discover something on two different parts of the planet at the same time. Knowledge is passed at a high level, so if two keen individuals are focused on the same quest, then one person's knowledge will impact the other's and vice-versa.

If the two strangers have no common interest, then the subsequent reaction will be small, not enough to cause conscious awareness.

## 2. Family Members - not close

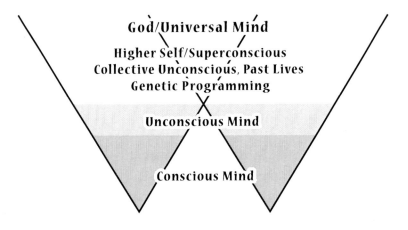

In Figure 2, family members share the same genetic space/collective unconscious space and universal space. While they may both have red hair, they may have little else in common. However, if they both have emotional issues and one person does therapy to release the low-energy emotions, subsequent generations sharing the same genetic coding will benefit by having the low-energy memories erased from the genetic material, as emotions are the realm of the unconscious mind.

An excellent example of this is a young woman of 19 who attended the same intense therapy week as me. She was screaming that she was being raped. It turned out that she was experiencing her grandmother's rape at the same age by guards in a concentration camp. The residual memory had survived in her grandmother's genetic material and been passed on to the girl. Through the regression work I've done with clients, by experiencing the trauma and releasing it, the girl will not pass on residual patterning to her own children, unless it is a very mild version.

This 'genetic memory' imprint can also be the reason 'false memories' can be uncovered by some regression work, as perhaps some long forgotten genetic memories surface and are mistaken for current life memories.

### *3. Close Family members/friends/daily contacts/workmates*

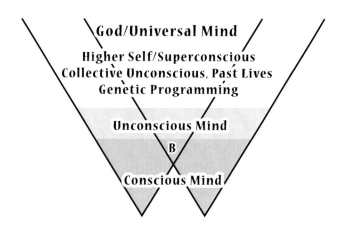

In figure 3, the common area can also include unconscious and conscious, as well as collective/upper and universal unconscious. This explains why the people we meet on a physical level, whether simply as acquaintances, or co-workers, or lovers act as our mirror (space B)!

By sharing the same space physically, we observe our own least and best qualities, explaining why we love people who are just like us and why we can dislike intensely someone who is – just like us! Every person you meet is a wonderful opportunity to discover something about yourself.

# The Power of the Spirit

## Human Energy

How can you connect with and harness the power of the spirit so that you can direct the energy into channels of creativity? All you are and all you see is energy. You are simply a series of energy fields; a play of light and shadows. The energy has different degrees of speed and density and it permeates and emanates throughout and outside the physical body. Your physical, mental and emotional body takes in universal energy through the top of your head.

You have seven main energy centres within your body. Each energy centre is called a 'chakra' or energy wheel. They are situated in the ductless glands of the endocrine system. The delicate balance of the autonomous nervous system is affected by the stability of the endocrine glands. The slightest fluctuation caused by an imbalance produces a disruption which will affect the whole organism.

As the light enters though the top of the head, imagine the body as a prism which refracts light into seven rays, corresponding to the seven colours of the rainbow. Each ray is attracted to one of the seven centres, becoming denser as it makes its way to the base of the spine, where the energy is slow and heavy. This base energy is called the Kundalini (sleeping serpent). Its corresponding colour is red. As well as a colour, each chakra in the body has an associated shape, sound and planet. A variety of emotions and illnesses appear when a chakra is out of balance.

It is the responsibility of the individual to integrate, mix and refine the energy, raising it upward through the seven chakras in order to harmonize the power and achieve a higher spiritual level. Meditation is one of the tools which can be used to raise the Kundalini energy, as can yoga, tai chi and other Eastern systems that control and use the breath.

Images which you will see during meditation are associated with the development of a particular energy centre. The images are similar to those we associate with dreams, although sometimes, when the meditation is deep and the timing is right, 'reality' can seem to be the real dream.

## *Exercises to Increase Psychic and Physical Energy.*

1) Sit with your back straight, head erect, as though someone is pulling it up with a piece of elastic. Imagine above your head a beautiful sun, or the light of God, shining clearly.

a.) Inhale to the count of four, breathing in the universal light energy through the top of your head.

b.) Exhale to the count of 11, imagining as you do the rays of light flowing into your heart centre (the middle of your chest) and expanding out of your body to the stars.

2) Increase energy by tapping your thymus area (in the centre of your chest, just below the collar bone) with your eyes closed while thinking of a time you were very happy or of someone you love.
Breathe.

3) Left hand flat over thymus, right on top of left. Imagine your heart opening like a flower and expanding pink energy to reach both hands. Breathe.

4) Tapping* opens the energy channels, removing energy interruptions. Tap all fingers on the chest, just below and to the left of the throat seven times. Using 3 or 4 fingers, tap between the eyebrows in a T shape and along the cheekbones below the eyes.
Cross both arms as though hugging yourself and tap both sides behind your armpits.
Tap the 'karate chop' spot on your hand to calm and energize you (the place you would make contact if you did a karate chop!).

5) To obtain an optimum state of wellness, imagine a holographic image of yourself standing in front of you. If you wish, you can imagine this image on a computer screen. Now observe the image turning around as though on a turntable. Notice that it is exactly as you want to be; perfectly healthy, slim and fit. Close your eyes and breathe energy into every cell of your holographic body as you feel, see or imagine  the body aligning itself with the blueprint of perfect health and functioning. Imagine an exact date sometime in the next few days or in the next month when you know that

*EFT – (Emotional Freedom Techniques) www.emofree.com

it's possible for you to look like the image in front of you.

6)  For spiritual healing, to release any low-energy feelings, repeat over and over in prayer, just before sleep:
"I place it in the hands of God." ('it' being whatever the issue is!)
"I place myself in the hands of God."
"I am one with the oneness."
You can replace 'God' with 'the Universe', or whatever works for you.

## Meditation/Visualization to Clear and Balance the Chakras
## (energy centres)

Record the following into a tape recorder, replay it, close your eyes and listen:

*It's a beautiful spring day. You are alone in a cabin in the woods by a calm blue lake, surrounded by trees and mountains. The air is crisp and clean outside. There's a fire burning in the grate and you can smell the wood smoke. It's a warm, comfortable place.*

*Warm your face and body in front of the open fire as it burns. Watch as the red flames flicker around pine logs, and smell the rich scent of the pine as the logs are consumed by the red fire. Feel the heat relaxing your body and take a deep breath of the red energy of the fire. Take the red to a small spot at the base of your spine and breathe out the rest.*

*Find a basket of oranges on the hearth next to the fireplace.*

*Take one of the oranges and feel its round, rough skin. Smell it and then dig your fingers deep into the flesh. Feel the juice drip down over your hands and fingers and suck the juice down into your body to a small place just below your navel. Leave a small spot of orange energy there and breathe the rest out.*

*Stand up and walk towards the door of the cabin. As you open the door, the morning sunlight streams in. Feel its warmth on your face and take a deep breath of the yellow sunlight. Breathe the light down to your solar plexus, between your ribs and above your navel. Imagine the yellow energy expanding throughout your body as you continue to breathe in the yellow sunshine.*

*Find yourself walking down to the lakeshore along a path. The trees on either side of the path are just sprouting bight new green shoots. As the trees diminish and you come to a clearing in the front of the lake, the new spring grass greets you. Breathe the green into the centre of your chest, leave a small spot there and breathe out the rest.*

*As you look up at the sky, the pink streaks of morning are still clearing. Breathe in the pink and take it to the very centre of your chest, inside the green. Leave a small spot there and breathe out the rest.*
*Blue water. Blue sky. A breathtaking view of mountains in the distance, towering over the majestic blue lake, gleaming in the morning sunshine. Breathe in the blue, listen to the birds sing and take the blue energy to a place in the centre of your throat. As you breathe out the rest of the blue, breathe the word "Haaah!" Become aware of the beauty of the purple mountain and take a deep breath of purple energy across the lake deep into your lungs and up to your forehead. Breathe out the remainder of the purple energy.*
*As the sun climbs in the sky, sit down by the lake and absorb the beauty of nature; the feeling of oneness with the universe. Relax, let everything go and just be in the moment as you sit on a rock or a log, feeling the presence of a greater power.*
*The mist which rises from the lake and surrounds the base of the trees winds its way softly around your feet. Take a deep breath of the mist; breathe it up to the top of your head in a counter clockwise direction then release it with a deep sigh. Let go of less than useful ideas, old beliefs and thoughts and know that you do not need to search for that which you already are: truth, beauty, and knowledge.*

✶✶✶✶✶✶✶✶✶✶✶✶✶✶✶✶✶✶✶✶✶✶✶✶✶✶✶✶✶✶✶✶✶✶✶✶✶✶✶✶✶✶✶✶✶✶

When you meditate, find a quiet place in your home to do it. As far as body position is concerned, the only thing to remember is to keep your back straight, so that the energy centres are aligned. If your home is not always tidy(!), have at least one area of your home tidy and spacious so that you can feel free to just relax there.

Now that you've learned about how your mind works, found your self-worth, cleaned out your physical body, cleared the old interference patterns, learned about communication with yourself and others and your connection with spiritual abundance is complete, it's time to manifest prosperity in the 'real' world.

# THE EIGHTH KEY
## The Power of PURPOSE and INTENT

Deepak Chopra\* explains that every cell in your body has neurotransmitters listening to every thought and communicating with every other neurotransmitter simultaneously. Imagine every cell in your body waiting in breathless anticipation for your next thought! Some of those thoughts are still out there in the universe searching for answers! Some of the thoughts and questions have answers and are waiting to return to you! They need a clear opening to get back, without interference caused by limiting beliefs and low-energy emotions and thinking.

Outcome thinking is the opposite of 'problem' thinking. It leads towards a solution rather than dwelling on what isn't happening. Change just for the sake of change just stirs energy around, rather like throwing a pebble in a pond. To really make things happen, you need to get in the boat and row downstream towards a specific goal or place!

Remember too that learning creates change, so another way to start to change is to sign up for a course. All change takes place first at the unconscious level and then we become aware of it at a conscious level. Change, however, is not the end but the journey. It's a journey from a not very satisfactory present state towards a more pleasant desired state or outcome.

### What do You Really Want?

What is the one thing you've promised yourself for as long as you can remember? Now is the time to make a date and start planning it. Get ready to focus exclusively on what you want, every minute of every day to bring your success.

\*Quantum Healing: Exploring the Frontiers of Mind/Body Medicine

What is success to you?

Success means so many different things to so many different people that you need to be able to decide what's really important to you. Is it money? Prestige? Happy relationships? All of these? You need to know why you want changes to happen and be able to state your intent. Do you just want to change your job or do you need to change your whole career? Do you want a nice relationship or do you really want love, marriage and a family?

Money, love, wealth, health and happiness should be like air – more than enough for everybody for as long as they live. When you believe that there is always going to be more than enough money, love and happiness, it becomes a self-fulfilling prophesy. In fact, the very fact that you can imagine yourself in a happy, successful situation means that it is within your reach.

Let's open up your imagination so that the unconscious mind can respond. What would you do if you could have anything you wanted????
Do the following exercise to find out your hidden desires:

## *SUCCESS AND ABUNDANCE*

**I have $1,000,000…today…tax free!**

**I buy:**

1) Length of time I take off work:

2) The new work I do is:

3) I learn:

4) The people I give money to are:                    and the
                                                      amount is:

5) The charity I donate to is:                    and the amount is:

6) I  invest $_____, in stocks/stores/property/other_____

Benefits of having this amount:

**I have $5,000,000…today…tax free!**

**I buy:**
(assuming that I'd bought all the previous things already):

1) Length of time I take off work:

2) The new work I do is:

3) I learn:

4) The people I give money to are:                     and the amount is:

5) The charity I donate to is:                     and the amount is:

6) I invest $_____, in stocks/stores/property/other_____

Benefits of having this amount:

**I have $1 billion today…tax free!**

**I buy:**
(assuming that I'd bought all the previous things already):

1) Length of time I take off work:

2) The new work I do is:

3) I learn:

4) The people I give money to are: and the amounts are:

5) The charity I donate to is:                    and the amount is:

6) I invest \$_____, in stocks/stores/property/other_____

Benefits of having this amount:

# Results:

**\$1,000,000 page**
Everything you wrote on this page is totally within reach. Act on everything and initially downgrade each one to something affordable to begin manifesting.

Example:
1)  I buy: *two new houses and a new car*
    (One house and change my car)

2)  Time off work: *forever!*
    (Change your job now!)
    Time off work: *six months*
    (Do the same thing but look for additional work)

3)  The new work:
    (Start researching courses)

4)  I learn:
    (Start saving *now* and decide the earliest date you can begin)

5)  The people I give money to:
    (Do something nice for everyone you wrote down here (e.g. a shopping trip, a nice compliment, a bunch of flowers etc)

6)  The charity:
    (Give a small amount to the same charity)

7)  Investment:
    (Open a small savings account or take out an endowment or insurance policy)

On the $5,000,000 page you wrote down the possibilities within the next five years and on the $1billion page you wrote down your ultimate goal in life (if you couldn't think of anything, by the way, then start imagining!).

Is there anything you can aim towards doing within five years? Start planning now! The very fact that you can imagine something means that your unconscious mind believes it to be possible.

## Is What You Want the Same as What You Need?

Did you notice as you did the exercise on what you really wanted, that as you realized that all your wants were fulfilled (three houses, ten cars, a private plane, etc.) your thoughts started to turn towards making a lasting foundation for the future? Something that you could contribute towards that would make a difference to humanity?

Usually when I ask people what's important to them, money and a good relationship are at the top of the list. Actually, that describes more what they want than what they need. When I asked the children in my daughter's class (ten-year-olds) what is important in life, they only came up with three things – home, play and family.

Success happens when you feel fulfilled, complete and at ease. It's when you attract in loving relationships, abundance in the form of food, home and financial freedom. At the end of the day, success is not how much stuff you accumulate or how slim you are. Real success is based on peace of mind – on how people remember you and how happy you made yourself and others.

## Leap into Life – and Love it!

Life is easy when you focus on what you want and take action to get it

The life you are living is the result of everything you've thought or believed for years. You are the complete master of your destiny. So get ready to focus on what you really want.

I first learned to ski in my late twenties when I went to Austria. The instructor was taking a group of about ten of us down a very icy slope. We were all beginners and we had to learn on intermediate slopes, because there was not much snow around. The real learners' slopes were barely covered. The instructor's cries of "Mind zee ice!" rang in my ears as I side-slipped to negotiate the mountainside. Sure enough, as soon as I saw the ice, I landed on my bottom. Nevertheless, I enjoyed the experience; I was even quite proud of all the bruises.

However, every time I went skiing after that, I would bump my way down to the bottom of every slope, usually more on my rear end than on the skis.
I just figured that I must be more daring than the others. This went on every year until one year I was at Blue Mountain (Ontario) with friends and I watched one of the men go easily down the same slope that I had just tumbled down. I asked him, "What's the trick? How do you avoid the ice?"
"I look for the snow!" he replied. It sounds so easy when it's put like that doesn't it?

Success is more to do with values. Success for you personally will happen when your values are fulfilled. How to find your values? Go ahead and read the following list. Pick out your ten or so most important states or values. Go through quickly and allow your unconscious mind to pick out the ones that jump out at you.

Of those you've picked, which is the one that is absolutely essential to your well-being? If you had that top one fulfilled, which is the next most important? And the next? Order the values so that you have your top 5-7.

What you value or need is much more meaningful than what you want.

So what's important to you about life?...........

# Key Values and States

Ability
Abundance
Acceptance
Accuracy
Achievement
Acknowledgement
Adventure
Altruism
Balance
Beauty
Brotherhood
Charity
Children
Comfort
Communication
Compassion
Competence
Contentment
Conquest
Co-operation
Courage
Creativity
Culture
Dignity
Discover
Duty
Ease
Energy
Excitement
Fame
Family
Forgiveness
Freedom
Friendship

Fun
Glory
God
Goodness
Greatness
Growth
Happiness
Health
Honesty
Honour
Hope
Humility
Independence
Individuality
Innocence
Innovation
Integrity
Intimacy
Joy
Justice
Kindness
Knowledge
Law-Abidance
Leaving a Mark
Leisure
Love
Mastery
Maturity
Money
Nature
Originality
Patience
Peace of Mind
Pleasure
Popularity

Positivity
Power
Prestige
Pride
Privacy
Property
Prosperity
Purpose
Reason
Respect
Responsibility
Risk
Romance
Routine
Safety
Security
Self-Control
Self-Esteem
Self-Interest
Service
Sex
Spirituality
Strength
Success
Support
Surrender
Talent
Teamwork
Toys
Treasure
Trust
Truth
Wealth
Wisdom

Health needs to be somewhere near the top if any of the others are to materialize. Why? Because the prime directive of your inner mind is to keep you healthy and alive. If you are not looking after your health your mind will bring it to your attention ahead of everything else by making you unwell. It is the vital driving force which is propelling you forward.

## *The Power of the Mind: Visualization*

The power of thought is AMAZING!  A number of years ago, I really needed to sell a house, as my then relationship had broken up and the house we were living in had taken all our money to renovate. The money we didn't have was mounting, along with the low-energy feelings! The house, a beautiful Victorian barn with a cathedral gallery, stained glass windows etc., had been on the market since October with hardly any interest. It was now February (cold, wet, rainy England!). I sat down one day and decided to come up with a 'sell by' date.  It was the last possible date that I would want to be out of the house. I created a picture in my mind of a letter saying: "Congratulations! You have sold 'The Stables' for more than the asking price!"  The date at the top of the letter was Sunday, May 22nd.

March came and went. Easter came with still no luck.  We changed the realtor, and every time I saw the 'For Sale' sign I visualized my little scenario with the letter and imagined SOLD written right across the notice board.

Hoards of people came through the house, with no takers.  It was a beautiful building, but it was the kind of house suitable for only a small group of people; for instance, it had no land at the back, so it wasn't good for anyone with children.  Finally, one weekend in May a flurry of visitors arrived.  One man walked in, shook my hand and said "I'll offer you the full asking price – I love it.  I'm going straight to the real estate office to sign the deal."  I was thrilled.  "Quick, what date is it?" I asked my ex. "21st May", he answered. "Hey, quite good!  I was a day early!"

The next day, first thing, another man arrived to say that he also loved the house. "Someone has already offered us the full $120,000", I replied.

"I'll take it for $122,000" he replied "and I want to move in by the 1st of June" (only nine days away!). It was the 22nd of May and I had been offered more than the asking price! By the way, the original offer from the man on the

Saturday didn't happen.  He apparently never even went into the real estate agent's office.

Did I engineer that date and price?  Did I pick up something from the future, or did I plant the thought for the future? What does it matter?  The fact is that high-energy visualization really does work. Your unconscious mind thinks in imagination and pictures and when you see it, feel it, breathe it, taste it, touch it, smell it, and hear it, your mind truly believes your visualization to be reality and will lead you right to it. As a clairvoyant and psychic I constantly dip into the future and 'remember' future events. It's easy for me. The way to make it easier for yourself is to ensure that visualizations and goals are intense, realistic and big!! with a date and time that is believable to your conscious mind. Use your amazing, innate creative intelligence to create excellence and magic.

## *Future Dipping*
## *- Goal Setting*

You can do these exercises mentally as you read, or record the scripts and then visualize as intensely as you possibly can.

1)
Imagine that you are in your own private theatre, ready to watch a film that you're directing. Make the theatre as comfortable as you can. (plush chairs or sofas, luxurious carpet, etc.).  In front of you is the screen.  Use the remote control in your hand to turn down the lights and begin the theatre show.

Firstly, imagine observing on the screen flashes of the prequel of your own life in black and white. You may hear a voice say,
"And here it is: ---------------'s (your name) life so far!"
Quick clips follow of previous episodes in your life. Of course, like any great film it has drama and excitement (*pause*). Then listen as the voice asks, "What was learned? (*pause*) What was achieved? (*pause*) Is it time to move on now? What does the future hold? Stay with us as we look ahead now." Suddenly you observe yourself on the screen, laughing, looking happy and healthy, living in a wonderful space with people you love, working at something you love to do which brings you pleasure and others benefit.
A date appears at the top left hand corner of the screen. It's a day and a month in the near future, with the current year. It flashes on and off vividly. You

notice that the program in your hand has the same date.

Feel yourself being drawn into the screen. You know, when you get so absorbed in a movie that it feels like you're there, looking through your own eyes. Who is there with you, or are you alone? Brighten up the colours and feel what you can feel, hear what you can hear. Touch and smell and taste the moment as you tingle with excitement. Where is that feeling in your body? Is there movement in the film or is it more like a snapshot? Does it feel like freedom or fun or both? Stay there until it really feels like a solid experience.

Close your eyes and you find yourself back in the theatre, observing yourself happy and alive on the screen. Take a deep breath of satisfaction and smile inside. Just before the film ends, what's the last thing that has to happen which makes you feel that the story has a happy ending?

You may find yourself listening to people clapping with delight because it's such a great film. As the lights go up you may observe people congratulating you and patting you on the back, or shaking your hand.

2)
For this future event, decide on the time you want the event to occur. Remember to write an exact time – the day, month and year.
Close your eyes. Now imagine seeing yourself in a normal setting. Watch yourself as you pick up a letter from the letter box or mat.

1) Find yourself looking through your own eyes. Open the letter and 'pan in' the camera for a close-up.

2) Again, observe the date at the top of the letter. Then:
   "Congratulations!! You, ----------------(your name) have done it! You have _____ " (here you will write the event)
   > e.g. You won the lottery!
   > You sold your house!
   > You are engaged to the most wonderful person!
   > You have overcome all and been pronounced fit and healthy!
   > You got the job!

Imagine the scene unfolding and then dissociate from the picture as you look at yourself laughing and smiling as you move into your new house, or picture yourself on your wedding day, surrounded by your friends and family, or see yourself shaking hands as you are offered that great job.

Cross your hands in the centre of your chest and take a deep breath of release as you open your eyes.

Do this visualization once a day, preferably just before you go to sleep, so that your unconscious mind is programmed for high-energy results. Manipulation, by the way, does not work with this exercise, so if it is not for your highest good, it may not happen. For example, if you want to marry Tony or Jane and Tony or Jane is not interested, visualizing a marriage with him/her may not work (we all have free choice). So use your date as your key point. If Tony or Jane has not shown any interest by the date you envisaged, change the scenario to "Congratulations! You have just become engaged to the perfect man (or woman!) for you!" Put in a new date. By opening up to endless possibilities we often actualize much better than we ever dreamed.

# *Wheel of Fortune*

The Wheel of Fortune is a very powerful means of creating something wonderful and it works! Many thanks to Colette Baron-Reid (Canadian intuitive, recording artist and author) for this one:

On a piece of cardboard or Bristol board, section off parts, like sections of a pie chart, and give each part a focus. One area could be for family, another for health, your love life, one for travel and leisure, and of course, one for career or money or home. Draw a very clear boundary all along the edges of the board. This detail is very important: it acts as a 'body' or vessel thereby giving symbolic form to its contents. In each of these, paste pictures or drawings or actual photographs, perhaps out of magazines; things that you would feel symbolize the optimum conditions and results for that category.

**Write a date underneath each photo or drawing– sometime in the next 12 months.**

Add affirmations, detailed statements of what you want achieved and state them in the NOW, as if they had already happened. Put the Wheel of Fortune on a door or wall where you will see it everyday. Read this on a daily basis to help stimulate those thought magnets and keep them consistent. You will see results!

The first thing to do to bring about a change is to move around the energy. If you were looking for a job, you would not usually just sit there, hoping that someone was going to spot you and promote you. You would normally put some energy into change. You might contact agencies, look in the newspaper, ask friends. So it is if you want wealth. You also focus when you are job hunting on something which is going to give you more money to have a nicer home or better holidays or a new computer. In other words, you focus initially on WHY. Why do you want more prosperity? Begin with the end result, e.g., a new house, a new car, better job. You can then work backwards to the beginning.

## *EVERYTHING BEGINS WITH A THOUGHT AND AN INTENT*

## *Feel-Good Affirmations*

a) Glance through the following list of affirmations. Choose one which relates to an issue that you are handling right now. Repeat it aloud three times and as many times as you remember it that day.

b) Fortune Cookies without the calories! Photocopy the next few pages and cut up the individual sentences. Fold the slips of paper twice then place them in a basket or bowl. Choose one each morning, read it out loud and repeat it ten times that day. You can also paste these individual affirmations near a light switch, on a mirror or anywhere else that you look at or touch on a regular basis.

I NOW CREATE, DIRECT AND STAR IN THE PICTURE SHOW OF MY OWN LIFE.

IT'S EASY FOR ME TO BE RELIABLE, KIND AND GENTLE IN EVERY ACTION - TO MYSELF!

I AM READY TO STUDY SOMETHING NEW WHICH INCREASES MY CREATIVITY.

IT'S EASY FOR ME TO BREATHE WITH THE RHYTHM OF LIFE.
THE LIGHT INSIDE ME GUIDES MY WAY.

IT'S NOW TIME FOR ME TO BE A HUMAN BEING, NOT A HUMAN
DOING.

I AM THE CAPTAIN OF MY SHIP. I HAVE MY COURSE SET FOR
SUCCESS.

PROSPERITY WILL COME AS SOON AS I VALUE MYSELF.   I AM
WONDERFUL.

IT'S NOT POSSIBLE TO HAVE THAT WHICH I ALREADY AM:
LIGHT, LOVE, AND WISDOM.

IT'S EASY FOR ME TO FIND MY TRUE PURPOSE IN LIFE AND FOLLOW
ITS EXPRESSION WITH COURAGE.

MY BEST QUALITIES ARE MY WARMTH, MY UNDERSTANDING AND
MY THIRST FOR KNOWLEDGE.

IT'S EASY FOR ME TO RECEIVE, KNOWING THAT IT ALLOWS OTHERS
TO FEEL THE PLEASURE OF GIVING.

IT'S EASY FOR ME TO FORGIVE MYSELF AND ALLOW MYSELF
UNCONDITIONAL LOVE.

MY TRUE PARTNER IN LIFE IS MYSELF.  OTHERS LOVE TO BE WITH ME
BECAUSE I AM MY OWN PERSON.

IT'S EASY FOR ME NOW TO ACHIEVE BALANCE, INNER HARMONY AND PEACE.

IT'S EASY FOR ME TO VIEW OTHER PEOPLE WITH COMPASSION AND MYSELF WITH FORGIVENESS NOW.

I ACCEPT HEALING, CONTENTMENT AND UNCONDITIONAL LOVE INTO MY HEART. I AM ONE WITH LIFE.

IT'S EASY FOR ME TO EXPAND MY AWARENESS AND BRING LIGHT INTO THE LIVES OF THOSE AROUND ME.

IT'S EASY FOR ME TO DISSOLVE MY FEARS AND TRUST IN THE LOVE OF GOD AND THE UNIVERSE.

THE UNIVERSE SUPPORTS ALL MY NEEDS, WITH A SURPLUS.

IT'S EASY TO FIND THE CREATIVE POSSIBILITY IN EVERYTHING I DO OR EXPERIENCE.

IT'S EASY TO COMMUNICATE MY IDEAS WITH SKILL AND SELF CONTROL. I HAVE A RIGHT TO EXPRESS MY NEEDS.

TRUTH, WISDOM AND KNOWLEDGE ARE WHAT I AM, NOT WHAT I NEED.

I LOVE MY BODY. IT'S A BEAUTIFUL TEMPLE OF LIGHT AND LOVE.

IT'S EASY FOR ME TO INITIATE CHANGE.
CHANGE BRINGS ME PASSION, POWER AND SUCCESS.


IT'S EASY FOR ME TO SURRENDER TO CHANGE.  EACH CHANGE BRINGS ME AN OPPORTUNITY TO BE HAPPIER.


IT'S EASY FOR ME TO BELIEVE THAT I HAVE FREE CHOICE IN EVERYTHING I DO.


IT'S EASY TO TRUST AND BELIEVE IN MY OWN JUDGEMENT.
I AM POWERFUL.


IT'S EASY FOR ME TO RADIATE WARMTH AND VIEW EVENTS WITH HUMOUR.  LIFE IS FUN.


I CAN SUPPORT AND HONOUR MYSELF.  IT'S EASY FOR ME TO ENJOY SUCCESS.


LEISURE AND PLEASURE ARE MY RIGHT AND MY REWARD.


IT'S EASY TO ATTRACT IN THE PERFECT MARRIAGE PARTNER FOR ME. MY RELATIONSHIPS CONSTANTLY GROW AND IMPROVE.


I CANNOT CHANGE MY FAMILY.  I CAN ONLY CHANGE MYSELF AND MY OWN REACTIONS.  I AM THE MASTER OF MY OWN DESIRE AND DESTINY.


IT'S EASY FOR ME TO DISCOVER THE POWER OF COURAGE WITHIN MYSELF.

IT'S EASY FOR ME TO CONCENTRATE ON ENERGIZING AND FREEING MY PHYSICAL BODY.

IT'S EASY FOR ME TO EXPERIENCE ABUNDANCE ON EVERY LEVEL.

IT'S EASY FOR ME TO EXPRESS AND ENJOY MY INDIVIDUALITY.

IT'S EASY FOR ME TO ATTRACT PROSPERITY INTO MY LIFE NOW.

IT'S EASY FOR ME TO LOVE TO EAT FRESH, HEALTHY, FOOD.

IT'S EASY FOR ME TO FIND NEW OPPORTUNITIES WITH WORK WHICH BRING ME PASSION AND PLEASURE.

IT'S EASY FOR ME TO LOOK UPON ANY SITUATION AS A NEW OPPORTUNITY  FOR PERSONAL GROWTH.

IT'S EASY FOR ME TO GIVE OPENLY AND RECEIVE WITH GRACIOUSNESS.

IT'S EASY AND VALID FOR ME TO SAY NO.  I LOVE TO TAKE TIME FOR MYSELF.

IT'S EASY FOR ME TO WORK HARMONIOUSLY WITH OTHERS.  I CONSTANTLY ATTRACT INTO MY LIFE PEOPLE WHO WANT TO SUPPORT AND PROMOTE ME.

IT'S EASY FOR ME TO LIVE EVERY DAY WITH PASSION.  I AM PASSIONATE ABOUT PEOPLE, LIFE AND LOVE.

## Prosperity and Abundance Keys

### *Motivation*
### *Intention*
### *Action*
### *Expectation*
### *Gratitude*

Are you willing to create your wealth now? Action is the bridge between dreams and reality. It may not be comfortable for a while and it's only when you're growing that you are not comfortable, so welcome that feeling. Anxiety is simply your unconscious mind's way of letting you know that you need to focus more specifically on what you want.

Do you want a better job or a purpose that adds value to your life and others? Are you ready to be rich and successful? You know how to succeed. You've already been successful at something in your life. Rich and successful people are exactly like you, except that they have a different strategy. They plan and commit to their plan with the expectation of success, ready to change and adjust as they go. Successful people make 'mistakes' often and use them as feedback to show them what they need to know that they wouldn't have known otherwise. In fact, the quicker and more often you go the incorrect way, the quicker you can be successful! Use your own natural talents to bring you the success which is rightfully yours as you follow these keys for financial happiness:

1)  Love yourself. Walk, talk and act like a Prince or Princess. Look at yourself in the mirror every day and say: "Gorgeous!" The true foundation of money and prosperity is self-worth. Yes, I know that there are rich people who don't like themselves. However, you want to be rich and happy don't you?

2)  Model yourself on someone you admire or look up to who is successful (remember the story of Good King Wenceslas? The page trod in the King's footsteps to make it easier to walk through the snow). It's easier to copy a model than to create a whole new one. Stay true to your values.

3) Be passionate. Love everything you're doing all the time and when you're not loving it, take the lesson and learn from it.

4) "No thought lives in your head rent free" - Robert Allen
Pay attention to your thoughts and commit to clear thinking, clear intent and clear action. Choose to think and speak differently in the language of success to be a power magnet.

5) Play to win/win. Reach for the stars.
Make sure that everyone and everything benefits by your actions.

6) We all live and long for attention, so say daily: "It's time now for me to get attention in healthy, positive ways that constantly bring me passion and power."

7) Read motivational books, or listen to success CD's (go to my website for some great CD's on prosperity, self-worth and abundance!).
Live in a state of constant expectation of wonderful things happening.

8) Look out for new opportunities every day. Take action to make things happen.

9) Take chances and correct as you go along.

10) Enjoy the success of others who have made it.
You want others to wish you well when you have made it.

11) Surround yourself with high-energy, powerful people.
Join a golf/ tennis / fitness club where successful people go.

12) Find solutions.
Write down situations and then write down possible solutions or ways to make them easier. Make a decision to do one of them and just do it!
If no solutions are forthcoming, make a decision to think about it later and let it go for now. Trust your unconscious mind to come up with a solution.

13) Choose a business that you can run initially alongside your day job.
Most self-made millionaires have their own businesses or are involved

in sales and marketing.

14) Take a course in marketing, sales or leadership. You're always selling yourself whether you have a job, or work for yourself.

15) Ask for help. It gives someone an opportunity to feel great. Your gift to them is to allow them to give you a gift.

16) Be generous and kind to yourself every day. Be adventurous as you try on all the other emotions and states: joy, happiness, love, passion, power, kindness, fun and enjoyment.

17) Have fun making money. Go wild every now and again by splurging to give you the feeling of abundance.

18) Weed out your low-energy qualities as though weeding a garden. As you notice any less than admirable traits, switch them.

19) Buy property. Real estate is probably the best long term investment. Read Robert Kiyosaki – 'Rich Dad, Poor Dad'.

20) Promote yourself. Get the word out there about yourself and what you do or sell. Join the Chamber of Commerce. Go to big charity functions and mix with wealthy people. Advertise yourself initially without spending money on media advertising.

21) What goes around comes around; the more money you make, the more other people make as you employ more people to help you to make more money to help more people.

22) Spend time every day being grateful for what you have, for who you are and what you're achieving. Only you can make you happy.

## *When do I Begin?*

## *NOW! NOW! And NOW! Again*

The right time is always now. This is the most powerful minute of your life as you have the opportunity right now to make your future happen. Money is simply an exchange of energy; the more energy you spend to make it happen, the more success (and money) you receive back.

A pilot flying to Australia or Hawaii, once he knows his (or her) destination has to take off in a specified time slot, perhaps his ten or twelve minute allocation. The only thing which may delay him could be outside his control – the weather perhaps. He trusts that the engineers have checked and rechecked the controls, so he just does a quick run through of the systems. Then with the co-pilot there as a back-up, he takes off. He may even set out in another direction for a while to take advantage of favourable headwinds. He knows that there are no straight lines in nature. He then adjusts his speed and direction and goes onto autopilot, relaxing for a while, perhaps even sleeping. As the destination draws near, he takes over the controls again ready for a safe landing. When the course is well set and the goal stated clearly, only minor adjustments are needed at the end.

## 9 Daily Keys to Success and Happiness

Every morning as you awake you have a choice. You can choose to let the day just happen, or you can choose to direct and plan every new day and create it.

Key1

**Be motivated.** Wake up and spend the first half-hour anchoring a high-energy state. Remember all the most wonderful times of your life. Get up 15 minutes earlier to exercise, meditate, do self-hypnosis or listen to motivational CD's.

Key 2

**Focus** on what you want and need. Write down your 3 daily goals to make them real. Read them aloud to breathe life into them.

Key 3

**Create** new opportunities. Call people. Sign up for courses - especially something you would not normally study – belly dancing, rock climbing - get out of the box! Join the Chamber of Commerce and groups of people working towards something. Be creative. Make something. Decorate your house, have a makeover.

Key 4

**Prioritize.** If your daily list is long, do the three priority goals and then congratulate yourself when you get more than that done.
Observe any distraction techniques in the form of 'busy' jobs that you find yourself doing, or when you get involved in other people's dramas. Thank your unconscious mind for making you aware, and then get back to the plan!
Be self motivated.

Key 5

**Take time off.** Write 'ME TIME' in your diary for at least half an hour and take that time for yourself. Stretch for two minutes. Treat yourself to a special coffee or tea. Listen to music. Dance or have fun for five minutes.

Key 6

**Be productive.** Make one call you need to make. Pay one bill you need to pay. Do ten minutes exercise. Eat nine foods with different colours (as little brown food as possible). Thank someone. Praise someone. Remember that your unconscious mind thinks you're talking about yourself!

Key 7

**Be grateful** for three or more things. Gratitude is an expansive feeling that opens up the window to joy and manifestation. Be thankful for the sunshine, the birds singing, your home, your own skills and special people in your life. Ask yourself, "What am I thankful for right now?" on the hour every hour. If the answer comes back "Nothing" then thank yourself for the information and make a decision to go and look for something now!

Key 8

**Believe.** What you believe and perceive becomes your reality which you then perceive and believe! It's time to make a decision to believe in what's working and realize that there's something that may need changing if it's not!
Choose today to focus on life affirming language, high-energy attitude and success oriented actions. Consciously use high-energy words like success,

happiness, joy, optimism, laugh, prosperity and health in your everyday speaking.

Key 9

**Reward yourself and have fun.** Enjoy life. Before you sleep, ask yourself, "What did I do well today? What did I not do well? Why did I choose to create that? What reward did I give myself today? What can I do tomorrow that will make me happier? I'm so looking forward to a great day tomorrow! I love life."

## Create Your Whole New World

Successful people make lots of decisions and make them quickly. You take the feedback from whatever emerges from your decisions and decide what else you need to learn to make success happen. You believe wholeheartedly in what you are doing. You live your life with passion and power. To be truly successful, the results you produce (be they financial, emotional, physical or mental) benefit not only yourself but others around you (a win/win situation), including the planet.

You are accountable. You assume that, even if something is not your 'fault' you can still do something to rectify and change it, becoming totally empowered. Fear and doubt are emotions of the middle brain. The same emotions will inhibit success, as it is from the higher mind, the cerebral cortex, the mind of the imagination, where success originates.

You can believe that 'fate' or 'bad luck' intervene in life, or you can decide now that even if fate happens, you still have choices. You are either in harmony with God or the Universe, or not.

For one month (or your whole life) think of life's events as a mirror. If you meet someone who is angry, ask yourself what or who you are angry with. If you meet a successful, happy person, congratulate yourself. If things are not going right, ask yourself, "What lesson is this teaching me, or what lesson could I take from this? What else do I need to know?

**AND WHAT CAN I DO ABOUT IT RIGHT NOW?"**

This is the most important part, because being accountable means taking action every time so that you are always moving forward towards your success. Excitement and curiosity are qualities that I hope you will keep your whole life. Give everything in your life 100% and enjoy using these wonderful tools that bring you satisfaction and joy.

*"Make it so."*

JEAN-LUC PECARD - CAPTAIN, USS ENTERPRISE, STAR TREK

# THE NINTH KEY
## The Power to CHANGE THE WORLD

## It's Time.....

to affect change in every part of the world, beginning with yourself.

It's time to make a difference now, because every word you speak, every thought you think, is resonating and vibrating throughout the world. It is on some level affecting every person on the planet. As you begin with yourself, by clearing your thought and speech patterns, your life choices will open as though by magic.

I always used to wonder why my own and other people's guides use telepathy to communicate. Now I know. It's because there is no interference pattern of negativity or limiting beliefs on the level of spirit or higher consciousness, so thoughts can be transferred easily. We have invented televisions and radios that pick up pictures and sounds in real time, when the signal is clearly transmitted. Our brains are so much more powerful than our technology.

You've transferred thoughts yourself. You've been thinking of someone and they phone you, or your thoughts keep drifting to someone and you find out later that they were not well or not feeling good. Have you ever noticed that the more congruent you are with someone, the more comfortable, the less need there is for language?

The more congruent you are with yourself, the more easily your thoughts will pass through the vibrational energy all around you. Whoever is on the same vibration will then be able to pick up on your thoughts as quickly as you think them! Thought 'manipulation' would not work, because manipulation is a middle brain process and would not be able to access the higher vibration needed to communicate the intent. Because manipulation is low-energy intent, it would set up an interference pattern, producing inconsistent results. Fear would be the 'conductor' by the recipient, who would again be using middle brain mechanisms and a low-energy pattern.

Once we all realize that by speaking, thinking and acting clearly, with high-energy intent, we will develop the rest of the cerebral cortex to the extent that our future becomes now in reality just by thinking coherent thoughts in a directed way. Your thoughts become like laser magic, achieving great results as you think with high-reaching intent and clear language. This is a powerful and positive way to live your life because success and happiness then become self-maintaining.

An interesting and thrilling development happened as I came to the end of writing this book. I had been using Keyspeech to change my language and my life for about eighteen months, with amazing success. I began waking up every morning with a sense of excitement and empowerment. People now telephone me or e-mail me almost as soon as I formulate a thought, with solutions to my questions and people's names to contact, without any conversation having taken place! I find my emotions appear and clear like a child's; flashes of emotion followed by feeling great in minutes, not hours or days.

Katie of course is an expert, as are some of her friends. They have so few low-energy words in their vocabulary as they are so young that it took just weeks to change their language patterns completely. They spot a low-energy word instantly. They mention that they don't feel at all good physically when they hear low vibration words being used.

I was wondering about how long it might take to change an older person's speech pattern. Will has taken longer to transform, yet his Keyspeech is improving daily. It seemed that it might take longer than I hoped to change the whole world's language so that we can succeed in creating world peace! Then something strange happened.

Will's sister Ann (from England) came to stay for two weeks. As we drove to the house she talked about how 'hard' the journey was. The flight was not 'bad', although the airline staff were very helpful. I could see Katie out of the corner of my eye wanting to speak to Ann and told her not to say anything as Ann didn't know about clearing her language. In fact, we popped right back into using low-energy words we hadn't used for months! For the first few days we explained to her why we speak differently and say "Switch" to each other. Then we carried on as usual. The second week my family spent a lot of time together. That was when I suddenly realized that when we were all together Ann used Keyspeech perfectly. There was not one low-energy word in her vocabulary! I know she's bright; however there was no way that she could have learned it that quickly. Then I remembered Sheldrake's Morphic field, which states that when one person learns something, the information can be transferred to the rest of humanity in the same instant using the unique hidden variable at the level of the quantum field. I remembered that I'd seen this once before and been amazed by it. Jade, our black standard poodle, had ten puppies and I felt amused as I watched one of the puppies, who was determined to climb over the plastic safety gate. She tried every day for three weeks. None of the other puppies were interested. They were playing with each other, or looking for food or love. One day she did it! The gate was two foot high and she managed to climb over by using the holes in the pattern of the gate to lever herself out. It took less than ten seconds for every puppy to be over the same gate. This is Sheldrake's theory in action!

I am in awe of how instantaneously this information channel opens up when the intent is strong. It is clear that the power of intent is the difference between succeeding and not succeeding.

In 1993, 4000 people meditated on peace for seven weeks in Washington DC. The study was monitored by sociologists and criminologists from leading universities and representatives from the police and government departments. Variables such as weather, daylight hours and time of year were taken into account. The results were astounding: violent crime and assaults went down by as much as 23% in the final week of the project, when the size of the group was largest. The statistical probability that this could reflect chance variation in crime levels is less than two in a billion.

For the past five years in over 50 centres around the world, the Global Consciousness Project (GCP) has been recording, on a network of devices sensitive to human mental and emotional frequencies, the variations and fluctuations that occur when huge numbers of people are focused on the same event, such as 9/11. Variations in this fluctuating force occurs when large groups of people are focused on world events such as disasters, celebrations or events that stir human thoughts and feelings. The GCP wants to learn about the global presence or consciousness. Research scientists are based in Princeton University in the U.S. and other parts of the world (e.g. Britain and Germany).

Dr Roger Nelson, the Director of the Global Consciousness Project at Princeton University, says, "In my global opinion, humans just don't stop at their skin. Consciousness is bigger than the physical body and… we have good evidence that there's an interaction of consciousness with physical systems."

At Princeton, in over 20 years of controlled experiments, scientists have found that people can influence random events by using their intention. Long distance healing has been proven to work in many studies. How wonderful to control and direct healing thoughts as gifts to help others. When every one of us is passing knowledge, love and light to everyone else, then the words of the song will come true:

"Then peace will guide the planet and love will steer the stars.
  This is the dawning of the Age of Aquarius"

World peace may be much nearer than we realize because of the quantum possibilities of the development of the neocortex. When global consciousness reaches critical mass, freedom is near.

It's time to bring the gift of awareness to everyone by teaching and passing on what we have learned. It's time for kindness to everyone, including ourselves and the planet. It's time for generosity of heart and mind.
It's time for confidence and hope.

The present is the only time we have to change the future.

## We are all One

## *Fast Forward to a Brighter Future*

(You might want to record the following script and listen to it every day):

*Perhaps you can allow yourself to close your eyes and…relax. You're breathing more deeply and more slowly… feel a beautiful, all encompassing light, which flows through your body with every breath you take.*

*Imagine yourself on the side of the most majestic mountain.*

*There's a light breeze playing with your hair and the air smells fresh and clear. As you settle down now you may become aware of the sound of water bubbling from a nearby spring. You know that it will taste delicious.*

*The view from here is endless…as you look at the far horizon you can see fields and valleys, green trees and a beautiful blue sky …*

*There's a soft morning mist that falls damp against your skin. As the sun gets higher, fe...e...e...l the warmth enter your whole body and …just …let …go.*

*Absorbing the sunlight through every pore, cell, organ and tissue of your lovely body … now or in the next few minutes. As you take a deep breath, then release it, you may still hear the sound of my voice in the background but you don't have to listen to the words, because your (you're)…unconscious  mind will hear and understand anyway.*

*In the background as you …breathe easily now on the mountainside, you may hear birds singing… and any outside noise will simply make you sli...i..i.de further .. and further into the most deep, relaxing state you've ever been in… in your life.*

*As the gentle sunlight warms your scalp you can feel it flow over your face and soften it, loosening the jaw and …releasing. The muscles around and behind your eyes are totally relaxed, because you're ready to just……be happy. The light brings with it a sense of peace, love, truth and harmony. With every breath, with every beat of your heart, you may allow yourself to go deeper and deeper into relaxation. That's right.*

*You can feel the warmth enter your neck and shoulders, like liquid light making its way down through your arms to your fingertips ..and one hand may feel different from the other as they loosen up further now.*

*As the light moves over and through your heart, your lungs liver and stomach, feel every cell heal and relax. The light goes through your hips to your legs, down through your knees and calves and into your feet, where you may feel a tingling as the sun renews every cell in your physical body with a healthy and new vitality. Become aware now, of your legs. As you think about them, notice that they seem to be getting v...er…ry relaxed. I will count down from 5-1:*

5,4,3,2,1. Logically you know that if your legs are 100% relaxed,
you just can't move them. So when you absolutely know that your legs are
100% relaxed, try to lift them ……(pause) …You can stop trying now.
And now bring your awareness up to your eyes. Your eyes are closed and the lids
are getting heavier and heavier. It seems that all the tiny muscles
behind your eyes are relaxing now. And if the eyelids flicker that just shows that
they are relaxing further now.
Relaxing your eyes one hundred times more than your legs, only when you're truly
convinced that the eyelids really won't work, try to open them. You may find to
your amusement that you cannot. (pause)
And now, stop trying and just relax.
As your awareness expands, take in the feeling of safety that this wonderful space
in nature brings to you. Now find the most safe, sacred place that you have in your
physical body and just take your attention to that area. Or just imagine where
that would be if you need choose a place. Feel the light and warmth flow into that
area and imagine a swirling vortex of energy spreading outwards from the safe
source. As you allow the light to expand, you may feel that the energy is increasing
with power.
You are expanding your awareness to the scene around you, to the mountaintop
and sky…and you may recognize that you are a part of that light; in fact you are
that soft, safe, all encompassing light. You can do anything. …You can be
anything you want to be…… You can be rich , happy, healthy and successful if
you ….give yourself permission now. You may feel an acceleration of learning as
you integrate the changes and allow yourself to preserve all the new learning that
is taking place now.
You may have a new perception of yourself and be surprised at your new capabil-
ities upon awakening. Your unconscious mind is in touch with everything and
everyone you need to know and ready to bring you great opportunities to have a
dynamic, compelling future. In fact, it's already experienced that wonderful
future, because it has the ability to observe as though seeing it from the top of a
mountain.
You know that you are already different from just a few moments ago because you
are far more relaxed, more aware, more ready to integrate and accelerate all the
new changes taking place. As you can notice those changes…the deep breathing,
the feeling of relaxation… now's the time to recognize that your subconscious
mind works perfectly. You realize that you can now safely release any limiting
decisions or low-energy beliefs you once held about being happy, healthy and
wealthy.

*Remember when you were younger? Remember what it would feel like to …wake up every morning with that new sense of wonder and excitement, feeling great, just as you did when you were a small child? In fact, you were born with an optimistic nature ……with a thirst for knowledge …even before you had conscious awareness.*

*Your brain processes two million pieces of information every second, so you can change your mind with the speed of thought. Your inner mind loves to learn and integrate new ideas...finding solutions to erase and transform old patterns into new, dynamic action that brings you forward into joy.*

*Deep breathing allows your brain to work more efficiently, so as you take a deep breath……then release it, feel yourself going deeper …and deeper ……inside to make the changes necessary to take you to a high-energy, dynamic future full of laughter and love.*

*The results are immediate as you… notice how relaxed you feel.*

*Your unconscious…mind is far more capable of making changes than you ever imagined possible. You can now accept and let go what cannot be changed and change what can be changed immediately as you awake. You may feel your chin lift and your shoulders release as you …realize how well you are doing.*

*You are now at a crossroads and you know that there is only one path to take… the one that is marked: Optimism and Action! Yes,… you can hope. Yes,… you can dream. Better still, you can take action as you awake to realize your hopes and dreams. This is the day you discover the authentic you. The beautiful, powerful person who still has the potential for joy and happiness that the tiny child has.*

*Imagine yourself expanding your awareness to a place just above your physical body, then observe a river of time leading back into the past.*

*As you float above the river, notice how clear and sparkling the water appears to be. Colourful fish darting in and out, luscious greenery on the banks. Find yourself relaxing as you become part of this lovely scene; a scene as old as time itself. You learned many lessons as you traveled along this river – some of them perhaps not to your liking, some of them thrilling and exciting. All of these experiences are now part of your unconscious mind, giving you vast amounts of innate knowledge about life itself, allowing you to…… create new behaviour patterns… now.*

*Observe a shaft of sunlight shining down onto the river like a spotlight …far, far back into the past …back to the source of all light and life. Travel back into the source, back to the oneness. Watch and feel and listen as the river lights up with the glory (of God). Glinting and reflecting on the past, carrying the light as it flows back to the present, dazzling and clearing any or all darker or dull memories as it returns to the present. The gift which is you today.*

*As you finally feel the warmth of the sun, float back down into your physical body. And now, remembering back to the most wonderful happy moment of this life-time... a moment when you feel truly connected......perhaps with a person, or with a scene in nature or just a moment when ...you feel totally in control.*
*How old are you in the memory? ............(pause).......................*
*Bring back to your conscious mind a symbol which represents that happiness .. perhaps one which will make you smile...It will be as easy to you as breathing as easy as making your heart beat, to remember that symbol many times every day, after you wake up. Anytime in the future that life is not as easy as you would like, you can instantly remember this symbol and smile, knowing that it originated in the past and can be repeated again in the future.*
*As you begin to become aware once more of your beautiful body, ask yourself: How..... ...I can change. How ....I can reward myself every day for the effort I put into life. How can I compel myself to succeed and win?*
*How can optimism and flexibility become part of my new approach to life?*
*Searching for solutions will become part of the excitement for you using the resources and skills which are second nature to you because you have reconnected with the beginning.*
*Your body, mind and spirit are synchronizing, harmonizing and integrating as you listen ..and your inner voice is telling you now that ...you are perfect.*
*Now that you are aware of a new feeling of understanding and intelligence you may even decide that you can preserve all learning, past and present, which serves to make you rich, happy and healthy.*
*Every small change that you notice will reinforce the belief that the work you are doing is paying off both emotionally and financially.*
*As you awaken you may become aware of a deep feeling of satisfaction; a security and a certainty that you are already on the path of change.*
*Your perception of who you are feels different somehow, as though you are more connected with the source of your security, which will come about through the changes you are ready to make immediately, as you awake.*
*In the days ahead, you may be surprised to find that you are holding your head and chin up more. You seem taller somehow...... more confident, as you take strong positive steps towards your dynamic, wonderful future. At least twice in the next two days or the next week you could find someone commenting on how different you look...how much happier you appear to be. It's amazing to you that all the people you know seem to like you more ...you like yourself more.*
*With every breath you take you are discovering wonderful things about yourself and with every discovery you are experiencing a deeper and more profound sense*

*of satisfaction with your life.*

*As you awake you are fully alert, ready to quickly complete any work which just seems to effortlessly flow from you.*

*Tonight you will go to bed and have the best night's sleep you've ever had.........dreaming, integrating, remembering......discovering...(repeat again and again in a whisper)*


*You will awake in the morning feeling the best you've ever felt...amazed at how easy it is to ....retain everything you are learning ...healthy, free, wonderfully refreshed and excited about your bright, compelling future where you are rich, happy, healthy and loving it......*

*As I count backwards from five you may find an amazing sense of joy inside you as you open your eyes.*

*Five... feeling that life is worth living with passion and power*

*Four...loving the new you*

*Three......More aware of your feet, legs, body and arms*

*Two... becoming clear-headed and fully conscious*

*And as you see hear or feel the number one in your head in the next thirty seconds, only when you are truly committed to being happy, open your eyes, feeling great.*

# The Breath We Share

*"Did you know that the average breath you breathe contains about 10 sextillion atoms, a number which, as you may remember, can be written in modern notation as 10? And, since the entire atmosphere of Earth is voluminous enough to hold about the same number of breaths, each breath turns out, like man himself, to be about midway in size between an atom and the world- mathematically speaking, 10 atoms in each of 10 breaths multiplying to a total of 10 to the power 44 atoms of air blowing around the planet. This means of course that each time you inhale you are drawing into yourself an average of about one atom from each of the breaths contained in the whole sky. Also every time you exhale you're sending back the same average of an atom to each of these breaths, as is every other living person, and this exchange, repeated twenty thousand times a day by some four billion people, has the surprising consequence that each breath you breathe must contain a quadrillion 10 to the power 15 atoms breathed by the rest of mankind within the past few weeks and more than a million atoms breathed personally sometime by each and any person on Earth...*

*"With such information you can more easily accept the fact that your next breath will include a million odd atoms of oxygen and nitrogen once breathed by Pythagoras, Socrates, Confucius, Moses, Columbus, Einstein or anyone you can think of, including a lot from the Chinese in China within a fortnight, from bushmen in South Africa, Eskimos in Greenland... and, going on to animals, you may add a few million molecules from the mighty blowings of the whale that swallowed Jonah, from the snorts of Muhammad's white mare, from the restive raven that Noah sent forth from the ark. Then to the vegetable kingdom, including exhalations from the bo tree under which Buddha heard the Word of God, from the ancient cycads bent by wallowing dinosaurs in 150 million B.C. and don't forget swamps themselves and the ancient seas where atoms are liquid and more numerous, and the solid Earth where they are more numerous still, the gases, liquids and solids in these mediums all circulating their atoms and molecules at their natural rates, interchanging, evaporating, condensing and diffusing them in a complex global metabolism"*

GUY MURCHIE

*Life is not measured by the number of breaths we take but by the moments that take our breath away.*

AUTHOR UNKNOWN

# Speech Magic –Transform Your Life Using the Language of Success

Words and thoughts have vibration and power beyond your wildest dreams. As you clear the old patterns of low-energy thoughts, low-energy words, low-energy actions and limiting beliefs, you make connections with the power of life and can manifest everything you ever want or need. Unencumbered thoughts shine as light into the darkness.

Like the parable of the seeds falling on fertile ground, we owe it to our children to nurture our language, our communication and our actions.
It's Time.

To begin, live for today.
Act as though you are rich, happy, healthy, loved and special.
Because you are.

You began reading this book thinking you might learn something; you were simply remembering what you already knew. You may remember, as you recall your previous body's experiences, the distance you have already traveled to come to this point in your journey.

You are not traveling alone.  You are part of the great oneness of life.  You are not looking for knowledge or truth- you **are** knowledge, love and truth.

When awareness and consciousness come together, you must then know that you can never end – you are perfect.

You always were.

Shine out your light.
Here's to Your Happiness.

# Resource Section
## Recommended Reading

10,000 Dreams Interpreted . . . . . . . . . . . . . . . . . . . . . . . . . . . . . . .Ball, P

A Richman's Secret . . . . . . . . . . . . . . . . . . . . . . . . . . . . . .Roberts, K

Babies Remember Birth . . . . . . . . . . . . . . . . . . . . . . . . . .Chamberlain, D PhD

Body Language . . . . . . . . . . . . . . . . . . . . . . . . . . . . . . . . .Quilliam, S

Buffetology . . . . . . . . . . . . . . . . . . . . . . . . . . . . . . . . . . Buffett, M

Building Wealth . . . . . . . . . . . . . . . . . . . . . . . . . . . . . . . Whitney, R

God is my Broker . . . . . . . . . . . . . . . . . . . . . . . . . . . . . . .Buckley, C

High-energy Words, Powerful Results . . . . . . . . . . . . . . . . . . . . . . .Urban, H

Living in the Light . . . . . . . . . . . . . . . . . . . . . . . . . . . . . . .Gawain, S

Magic of NLP Demystified . . . . . . . . . . . . . . . . . . . . . . . . . . . . Lewis, B

Messages from Water . . . . . . . . . . . . . . . . . . . . . . . . . . . . ..Dr Emoto, M

Power vs. Force . . . . . . . . . . . . . . . . . . . . . . . . . . . . . . . .Dr Hawkins, D

Quantum Healing: Explore the Frontiers of Mind/ Body Medicine . . . . .Chopra, D

Rich Dad, Poor Dad . . . . . . . . . . . . . . . . . . . . . . . . . . . . . . .Kiyosaki, R

Secrets of the Millionaire Mind . . . . . . . . . . . . . . . . . . . . . .T.Harv Eker

Take Your Money and Run . . . . . . . . . . . . . . . . . . . . . . . . . . Doulis, A

The 12 Hour MBA Program . . . . . . . . . . . . . . . . . . . . . . . . . . .Sobel, M

The 17 Principles of Personal Achievement . . . . . . . . . . . . . . . . . . . .Hill, N

The 7 Habits of Highly Effective People . . . . . . . . . . . . . . . . . . . . .Covey, S

The Cure for all Diseases . . . . . . . . . . . . . . . . . . . . . . . . . . . .Clark, H

The Eternal Journey (near death exps.) . . . . . . . . . . . . .Lundahl, C & Widdison, H

The Field- Quest for the Secret Force of the Universe . . . . . . . . . . . . .McTaggart, L

The Footprints of God . . . . . . . . . . . . . . . . . . . . . . . . . . . . . .Isles, G

The Laws of Money and the Lessons of Life . . . . . . . . . . . . . . . . . . .Orman, S

The Master Cleanser . . . . . . . . . . . . . . . . . . . . . . . . . . . . . .Burroughs, S

The Prophet . . . . . . . . . . . . . . . . . . . . . . . . . . . . . . . . . . Gibran, K

The Secret Life of the Unborn Child . . . . . . . . . . . . . . . . . . . .Vernay, T/Kelly, J

The Secret of Creating Your Future . . . . . . . . . . . . . . . . . . . . . . .James, T

Think and Grow Rich . . . . . . . . . . . . . . . . . . . . . . . . . . . . . . .Hill, N

Through the Open Door- Secrets of Self-Hypnosis . . . . . . . . .La Bay, M/Hogan, K

Time Line Therapy and the Basis of Personality . . . . . . . . . . . . . . . . .James, T

Using Your Brain for a Change . . . . . . . . . . . . . . . . . . . . . . Bandler, R

You Can Heal Your Life . . . . . . . . . . . . . . . . . . . . . . . . . . . . Hay, L

Your Infinite Power to be Rich . . . . . . . . . . . . . . . . . . . . . . . . . .Murphy, J

# Infomercials
# www.hypnonow.com

## Breakthrough Body Kit
Yvonne's Breakthrough Weight-Loss/I Love My Body Kit -includes 7 CD's, Body Wizard Book, Keyspeech - Change Your Language Guide and pendulum to increase your metabolism. Great practical tips on cleansing and body image.

## Do It Yourself (DIY) Hypnotherapy Kit
For less than one hypnotherapy treatment you can learn and make your own personalized hypnotherapy CD's and tapes using pre-recorded tracks that will allow you to mix and match over 1000 combinations. Instruction book and background explanation included.

# Individual Hypnosis CD's (with Wonderful Original Background Music)
All tracks are around 20-25 minutes in length

## Abundance Now!
Abundance Now is an amazing dual hemisphere CD which accesses the unconscious mind directly so that prosperity and abundance become an automatic state of being and thinking. On Track 1 you hear two different voices (Will and Yvonne) at the same time; one talking to the conscious mind and one to the unconscious so that prosperity is accepted wholeheartedly. Track 2 is Yvonne's voice, with suggestions of abundance and joy.

## Relax into Prosperity
Relax into Prosperity is a delightful way to allow the unconscious mind to accept suggestions of new ways to feel about money and success. Two twenty minute sessions (one male, one female voice) take you on a wonderful journey to success and prosperity.

## Optimistic Thinking
Optimistic Thinking takes you forward to a brighter future. It is full of suggestions to help you live a whole, dynamic and passionate life! Uplifting and joyful.

## Goodbye Negativity
An amazing story told in metaphor to allow you to release the past negative emotions and limiting beliefs. Track 1- dual hemisphere. Track 2 – single voice.

## Clear the Stress
Breathe and release all stress from your body and mind. Relax into harmony and happiness with Yvonne's soothing voice. Beautiful background music.

## Release Those Cravings NOW!
It's time to let go of body cravings. Learn to crave exercise instead! 21 days will transform your life.

## Healthy Choices
Choose to change as you learn to automatically prefer fresh, healthy foods that will take you to a slim, healthy body and life.

## Forgive Yourself and Others
An adaptation of a Hawaiian Forgiveness technique. Go to a magical forest and release and forgive as you come to new understandings about the people in your life.

## Cellular Spark
Remind your body of its blueprint of perfect health as you transform your organs, tissues and bloodstream with messengers of inner light.

## Bring out the Magic Inside
Find the authentic you inside and create the new you of the future. Love yourself as you are – beautiful and complete.

## I Love my Body
This CD will transform the way you think about your body, step by step. Sensual and loving, you'll learn to enjoy every part of your beautiful body.

## Past Life Regression Guided Meditation CD
Have you ever wondered if you have lived before? ~ or questioned why you have the parents, friends and experiences that you've had in this lifetime?
This CD takes you a wondrous journey of the past, to reveal your hidden talents; to claim back your power so that your future will be lighter, brighter and more successful.

# Experiential Workshops

**Inner Magic – Outer Success** – The secret of success is self-worth. Learn to love yourself by releasing negative emotions and limiting beliefs. Set realistic goals for the future and see them come true.

**Do It Yourself Hypnotherapy Day** – This powerful one day workshop will enable you to write and record your own hypnotherapy scripts for a healthy, happy, prosperous life.

**Breakthrough Weight-loss Day** – Using the **Hypno Health Slimmer You Book,** great C.D's, a FREE pendulum and a BONUS Optimistic Thinking C.D. you will learn how to talk to your subconscious mind so that it really listens!

### *Learn to be a Hypnotherapist*

Yvonne teaches you to be a Board Certified Hypnotherapist. This wonderful tool enables you to help yourself and others using an ancient technique which has been accepted as a complementary modality to conventional medicine. Additional Classes: Hypno-anaesthesia, smoking cessation, weight loss, stage hypnosis.

Go to: **Yvonne@hypnonow.com** to invite Yvonne to speak or teach at your function or seminar. She is well known for her magical way of making everyone feel special. Her humour and knowledge will transform your world. **Or ask about** a personal breakthrough session using NLP, Time Line Therapy™ and Hypnosis. Great for permanent changes in relationships, career, prosperity, health and self-worth.

Telephone Yvonne NOW in Toronto at 416-494-2233.

## www.hypnonow.com

### With Special Thanks

This book is dedicated with love and gratitude to the two loves of my life, Will, my husband, and Katie, my daughter, for their total support and inspiration.

*Special thanks to:*
*Robert Doyle, for his brilliant mind and perceptions,*
*and Carrie Bailey and Colette Baron-Reid*
*who have my admiration for their passion for life.*

*My family, Mother Ruth, sisters Jen, Val, Treena and Ann,*
*for just being there for me.*

*Blessings to:*
*Elaine Charal and Sheena Gaidy, for their years of loyalty and assistance,*
*Karen Peterson and Joseph Luca for their generosity,*
*and to all of you lightworkers who are with me on the path.*

# Win Free Stuff!

## *Win a Free Seminar, CD or Workshop*

### *How to Enter*

Simply e-mail Yvonne@hypnonow.com with your comments about how your life or perspective on life has changed as a result of reading her book: Keyspeech – 9 Keys to Inner Power. As a thank-you gift, you will be entered in a monthly draw to win one of the following prizes:

- ♣ A fabulous, transformational one day Key to Inner Power seminar.
- ♣ A chance to choose a one evening workshop from the nine week course 9 Keys to Inner Power: A week-by-week in depth exploration on how to find and make your own magic formula for success.
- ♣ A Breakthrough Body Kit or Do-it-Yourself Hypnosis Kit.
- ♣ A Hypnosis CD of your choice.

You get one chance at this so act now!
Prizes will be drawn on the first day of every month and winners notified by e-mail.

## www.hypnonow.com

# Yvonne Oswald

**_MHt, MNLP, MTLT_**™

Internationally acclaimed Yvonne Oswald is one of the most renowned and respected facilitators in North America. She has a reputation for her exciting, innovative and interactive seminars. British born and a qualified teacher with 20+ years' experience, Yvonne helps every audience (live, radio/television) clear issues and quantum leap their personal growth and life choices.

She taught in England and South Africa, and then spent two years teaching English as a Second Language in Rome, Italy. After coming to Toronto, Canada, in 1989, she taught workshops at the Learning Annex for over ten years and regularly appears on local and national television and radio. She still lives in Toronto and is happily married with a lovely daughter.

As a board member of the Ontario Association of Hypnotherapists, she is committed to the continuing education of all its members and the promotion of personal empowerment.

A Master Clinical Hypnotherapist, Master NLP Practitioner, Master Time Line Therapist™ and certified in Hypno-Anaesthesia, Yvonne specializes in personal growth. She offers mini and full Breakthrough Sessions.

ISBN 1-41206400-7